T
Birmingham &
Aberystwyth Walk

by John Roberts

by walkers .....for walkers

****
WALKWAYS
John Roberts
67 Cliffe Way, Warwick
CV34 5JG   01926 776363
****

THE
BIRMINGHAM & ABERYSTWYTH
WALK

by John Roberts

ISBN   0 947708 37 5

First Published 2001

Engine Branch aqueduct, Smethwick

Arley on the River Severn

Above the Elan Valley

i

Contents

When I Was Very Young   1

Field, Forest, Mountain & Moor   2

Using the Guide   8

Amendment Service   10

Starting Points & Pubs   11

General Map   15

Walk Stages & Accommodation   16

Starting/Finishing at Stourbridge   17

The Birmingham & Aberystwyth Walk   19

When I Was Very Young

The idea of a Long Distance Footpath from Birmingham
to the west developed in the 1970s after much walking
in the Severn Valley and Wyre Forest. At the time there
were few Long Distance Paths in the Midlands. The Heart
of England Way was barely established, The Staffordshire
Way existed but the Worcestershire Way was no more than
a Territorial Army map reading exercise and the North
Worcestershire Path was just being planned.

Staring at all that virgin space on the maps, it seemed
perfectly clear to me that what the world really needed
was a walk west from Birmingham. I knew of mysterious
and wonderful places in a misty Celtic west. I knew wild
and silent hills, sullen lakes, frothing rivers and steep,
lost valleys. I knew all this as A E Houseman knew his
'blue remembered hills', that is, I loved the idea and
the feeling of these quiet landscapes as much as the
reality, and I wanted to share them.

The first version of this walk was published in the early
1980s in three separate A2 sheets, *Birmingham to Ludlow,
Ludlow to Rhaeadr (Rhayader)* and *Rhaeadr to Aberystwyth.*
They went out of print years ago and I have long wanted to
redesign the route and publish the whole thing in a single
book.

Overall, this is the same walk and visits the same places
but I have made important route changes to give a more
interesting and rewarding experience. My techniques for
describing walks have also developed since the 1980s and
I hope you will find the directions clear and easy to use.

John Roberts
Autumn 2000

Field, Forest,
Mountain & Moor

You can start the Birmingham & Aberystwyth Walk at
either end but I give this outline of the landscapes from
east to west. The profile shows the main rises and falls,
but the horizontal scale is more compressed than the
vertical so the hills are not quite as steep as they look.

The eastern end of the route is at Gas Street Canal
Basin in central Birmingham, which is a feature of the
rejuvenated area around Symphony Hall and the Inter-
national Convention Centre.

Starting or finishing an LDP with some 20 miles through
a heavily industrial urban area may not appeal to you, so
notes and route directions are given to enable you to start
(or finish) the walk at Stourbridge, on the western edge
of the Black Country. Even so, this is a fascinating and
rewarding walk through British history on quiet, secluded
waterways which are very green and often quite beautiful.

The walk sets out on the ruler straight Birmingham Canal,
passing through worn brick buildings and majestic cuttings
and crossed by handsome iron bridges. Several locks mark
slight changes of level but they don't register on the
profile.

After 7 miles the route leaves the canal to rise up a green,
open space leading over the Rowley Hills. At 255 metres
this is the highest point on the walk until you reach the
Clee Hills in Shropshire. This small range lifts you over
the major watershed between the River Tame, flowing
into the Trent and the North Sea, and the River Stour,
which joins the Severn to run into the Bristol Channel.
The views are huge and stirring, with tumbling valleys
of houses, factories, pubs, churches, shops and people,
against the ranges of western hills.

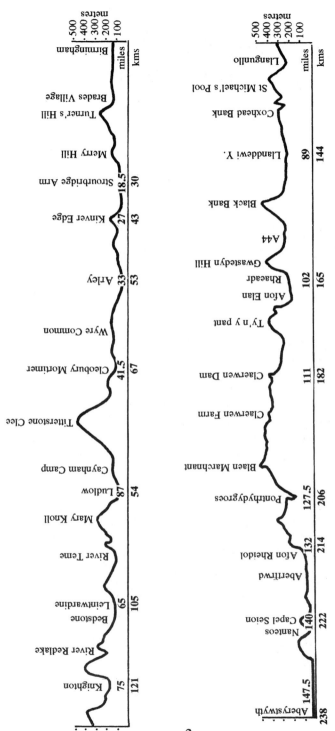

The distances are between the Starting Points; see
the list on page 10 and the map on page 15.

3

The walk drops to join the Dudley No. 2 Canal, a pictur-
esque waterway which loops and twists for miles through the
Black Country. Then quite suddenly you are out of town and
into wonderful country, with the tree shrouded canal curving
between low, green hills.

Leaving the canal the walk climbs and follows the long,
wooded sandstone ridge of Kinver Edge (180 metres), before
falling into a shallow valley and climbing again to the next
ridge. The countryside is well wooded, with small fields,
thick hedges and two big woods. In a couple of miles you
reach the edge of the Severn Valley and plunge down to
the waterside village of Arley, at 25 metres.

After a short, steep climb from the river you reach a plateau
at 90 metres and vanish into the Wyre Forest. The Wyre lies
across two north - south ridges and the land is also cut by a
network of north and south and west to east flowing streams,
producing a complicated landscape of small hills and valleys.
Here you reach about 150 metres. The Wyre is not all trees.
In one tranquil and forgotten green corner there is an interlude of open fields, isolated farms and sandy tracks.

Leaving the forest and dropping into Cleobury Mortimer
in the valley of the River Redlake (100 metres), there is
no dramatic change in the scenery, but the land begins to
look more sparse. There are fewer hedgerow trees, fewer
hedges, more wire fences, and the rises and falls become
bigger and simpler.

From Cleobury you cross a big dome of a hill to reach
Hopton Wafers, then start to climb through very different
country. The fields are rough grazing, there are reeds, the
trees are smaller, and as you get nearer to Titterstone Clee
the land becomes a harsh, infertile upland.

At 475 metres Titterstone is one of the three highest
points on the walk and gives a magical panorama of the
Shropshire and Welsh hills. But the hill itself is a mean,
hard forbidding rock which has been brutally quarried, a

wilderness of coarse, tussocky grass, abandoned spoil heaps and rusty wire fences.

The long, gradual fall into the valley of the River Teme at Ludlow (75 metres) is broken only by the small eminence of Caynham Camp (153 metres). This grassy arena ringed by earth ramparts may not seem high, but it commands the flat land of the valley and gives gorgeous views.

West from Ludlow is one of the grandest parts of the walk. Climbing from the river you enter the Mortimer Forest and a couple of miles on reach 298 metres at Mary Knoll. The long, straight stride towards Burrington gives entrancing views to the west.

We can't go straight down into the Teme Gorge and on to Leintwardine as common sense suggests. Instead there is a rewarding kink to the north to pass the romantic 18th century fantasy of Downton Castle and cross the Teme. A long descent through woodland leads into the charming riverside village of Leintwardine (120 metres).

This is where the River Clun flows into the Teme, and the next 4 of 5 miles crosses a low reedy area of small streams, ditches and alders. It is quite unlike any other part of the walk.

Rising slightly you reach Bedstone, which marks your first step over a series of fierce little hills bristling with pine and spruce. Instead of seeing their infinitely desirable grey outlines on the horizon you are in amongst them. This is the Welsh Marches landscape of forestry, sheep and magical remoteness.

At the little market town of Knighton you enter Wales, but the landscape continues to rear and plunge and has much the same character for nearly 30 miles. There are close cropped fields, small woods, forgotten farms, a small silted lake, a sweeping brackeny common, miles of lost, stony tracks and hardly a person.

South of Abbeycwmhir you pass through a forest with
some of the steepest contours on the walk. Pause often
as you climb to 480 metres and view the miles of misty,
blue hills. Then comes a glorious run downhill before
another climb up Gwastedyn Hill at 443 metres which
overlooks Rhaeadr, and a great deal more.

Rhaeadr stands on the Afon Gwy (River Wye) at 214
metres. There are several possible routes west but most
of them involve messy circuits of the Elan Valley Reservoirs without giving especially good views of them. I
decided to start on the Wye Valley Walk which runs
downriver for a couple of miles then climbs sharply to
a hilltop track. It gives a higher level walk which does
not itself give views of the reservoirs, but I have added
a small excursion which does.

After an exhilarating stretch through the hilltops, you
fall to follow the Afon Claerwen up its harsh valley to
the grim, grey dam. For the next 26 miles you follow
tracks and an unfenced road across some of Britain's
wildest moorland. I had expected the section by the
Claerwen Reservoir to be rather dull, but not so. The
valley is shallow and small rises and falls switch the
scene between water level and the open moor to give
a most rewarding walk. It is a safe, all weather route.

These moors are part of the Elan and Claerwen catch-
ments which were bought by Birmingham Corporation
for the water scheme. The Act of Parliament behind it
all provided that the land would be open to the public
in perperuity, so in this area we have had a 'right to
roam' since the 1870s. The only roamers off the well
marked tracks that I have seen have been on Army exer-
cises. How much use will be made of the wider right to
roam that the Rambler's Association has won?

After an interlude along an unfenced road the walk
takes to another long, winding track through the same
green wilderness. After several remote and abandoned

6

farms it reaches a gate and turns onto grass. There is a pleasant descent through rough fields into the deep, oak clad valley of Cwm Ystwyth.

Pontrhydygroes lies at 130 metres and for the next 2.5 miles you must toil up a rough, wet and ancient track through sheltering woodland onto a moor with a summit of 255 metres. Rising and falling more gently now, the walk continues to Pontarfynach, or Devil's Bridge.

Cwm Rheidol is a deep, steep, woody cleft between high and sumptuous hills which run over the horizon in all directions. A steep path leads down to one of our loveliest rivers at 90 metres and follows it for 8 miles, the little steam railway alongside. Then comes a sharp haul out of the valley at 30 metres to Capel Seion at 150 metres.

The rest is simple. A sharp drop to Nanteos Mansion at 46 metres, a climb through the parkland of the great house followed by upland fields to 181 metres, and then the last, long drop. From the steep, gorsey hillside you can see and smell the sea. The last 3 miles runs beside the Afon Ystwyth to a shingle bank facing the breakers.

Between Knighton and Rhaeadr

7

Using the Guide

The Birmingham & Aberystwyth Walk is my own invention and not the creation of any county council, so there are no special waymarks. Not yet, there aren't.

The **route directions** are quite separate from the description and comment, they are very terse, and set in short, narrow, numbered paragraphs in a clear and open typeface. My aim is to give information in easily located and remembered blocks of convenient size, bearing in mind that you will be reading them on the move.

Distances in *yards* or *miles* are to give you a rough idea how far to walk. You do not need to measure because you will be given something to look out for, such as a house or church. So if I say "go .5 mile to the old mill", you will not worry that someone has made off with it after 200 yards. I use yards where I think you will know how far I mean, but few of us know what 600 yards look like, so for longer distances I turn to fractions of a mile.

Distances in *paces* are given to be counted out. These are infrequent and only for a few yards at a time. Paces vary but you can allow for being tall or short. The reason for all this is that people carry a pace with them but not usually a measuring tape.

The **abbreviations** are obvious but certain phrases recur. You will see *half R* (or L) meaning a half turn, or about 45 degrees. Therefore *bear R* (or L) means a narrower angle than a half turn, or just tending away from straight ahead. A *road* has a tarmaced surface and a white line down the middle. *Lanes* are tarmaced but smaller and without white lines. *Drives* are the same but not public. *Tracks* are wide enough for four wheeled vehicles and might have an earth, grass or stone surface, but not tarmac. A *path* may have any surface, from mud to tarmac but is only pedestrian width.

A **compass** is not essential for this walk because landmark navigation is possible for the whole route, in daylight and clear weather. For those who can use one, a compass can be helpful in poor visibility and in certain places. I have given bearings where I thought they would be useful.

The **bearings** given are *field bearings* assuming in 1998 a magnetic deviation of 4 degrees west to the east of Knighton and 3 degrees west to the west of the town.

The **maps** are sketches to an approximate scale of 2.5ins/1 mile or 4cms/1km. Small numbers appear on them and these refer to paragraphs in the directions, the westbound route to Aberystwyth - eg (W33), and eastbound to Birmingham - eg (E41).

Many people like to carry **Ordnance Survey** maps and I list the relevant sheets. You should not need the 1:25,000 scale Explorers but the 1:50,000 Landranger sheets will help you find starting points more easily, and might be useful if you want to leave the route for an urgent dentist or something.

Landranger Maps (1:50,000) (1.25 ins/mile) (2 cms/km)
    139 Birmingham,
    138 Kidderminster & Wyre Forest
    148 Presteigne & Hay on Wye
    147 Elan Valley & Builth Wells
    135 Aberystwyth & Machynlleth

Explorer Maps (1:25,000) (2.5 ins/mile) (4 cms/km)
    220 Birmingham
    219 Wolverhampton
    218 Wyre Forest
    203 Ludlow
    201 Knighton
    200 Llandrindod Wells
    187 Llandovery (a corner)
    213 Aberystwyth

Amendment Service

The countryside changes all the time. Paths are diverted and hedges removed, there are new tracks, fences and barns, On the Heart of England Way some 15 changes occurred in one period of three years. To keep walk directions up to date I issue Amendment Slips - a unique and FREE service.

PHONE ME on 01926 776363 with a note of the books that you have and I will send you up to date Slips. EVEN NEW or recently purchased books can suffer changes within weeks.

PLEASE WRITE OR PHONE to report any changes or problems, stating book, route and paragraph number.

DON'T BOTHER copying changes into your book(s). Just dab affected paras with highlighter and keep the Slips in the front of the plastic cover.

Many people never ever use this service, its far too much bother for them.

The Country Code

* Enjoy the countryside and respect its life and work
* Guard against all risk of fire
* Fasten all gates
* Keep your dogs under close control
* Keep to public paths across farmland
* Use gates and stiles to cross fences, hedges and walls
* Leave livestock, crops and machinery alone
* Take your litter home
* Help to keep water clean
* Protect wildlife, plants and trees
* Take special care on country roads
* Make no unnecessary noise

Starting Points & Pubs

Listed below are the best places to join or leave the route:
see the map on page 15. The map reference and the place
described refer to the point (eg church, bus station etc)
from where the route directions start, which may not be
the centre of the town or village.

For each place I have given details of car parking space,
transport connections and various facilities. Accommodation is covered in the next section. Also listed are pubs
in between starting points.

ALTERNATIVE STARTING POINTS.

(1) **Birmingham.** The eastern end of the walk is at Gas
Street Canal Basin in central Birmingham and it follows
some 20 miles (32 kms) of canals and green open spaces
before reaching the countryside at Stourbridge. Read my
comments in *Field, Forest, Mountain & Moor.* I find it
exciting, dramatic and surprisingly attractive.

(2) **Stourbridge.** You can start from this town on the western edge of the West Midlands area and walk straight into
the country. See the next section for notes about travelling
to and starting the walk at Stourbridge.

(3) **Kenilworth.** If you are quite mad you could start further
east and walk the *North Worcestershire Path & Midland Link*
from **Kenilworth**. The *Link* is my own invention, the Path a
County Council job which joins the Birmingham & Aberystwyth Walk at Kinver Edge. It would add only 40 miles.

At each Starting Point the route directions are worded to
cater for people starting from there, and I show the paragraph numbers below. Walkers just passing through may
find the wording of directions at Starting Points a bit
odd or superfluous, but they will still be clear.

11

I have noted whether bus or train services exist at the Starting Points. Phone 0870 6082608 to find out times. You will get an operator covering your local region but can be transferred to others as necessary. Places between Birmingham and Leintwardine fall into the West Midlands region, for places in Wales ask for North Wales, not south.

Gas Street Basin (SP 062866) - canal basin in central Birmingham .5 mile from New Street Station. Get there by towpath or through an arch in a brick wall in Gas Street, off Broad Street. Ask for directions from bus or train stations.

(Pub) Brewer's Wharf, Merry Hill Centre.

(Pub) Prince of Wales (Ansells), Rounds Green.

(Pub) The Tenth Lock (Banks's), Nine Locks.

(Pub) The Old Bush (Hanson's), Brierley Hill.

(Pub) Samson & Lion (Marston's), Buckpool.

Stourbridge (SO 904843) (W26) (E327) - bus and railway station in Foster Street on outer side of ring road. All facilities.

(Pub) The Stewpony (Banks's), Stourton.

Kinver (SO 834846) (W29) (E324) - Olde White Hart Inn in village off A458 Kidderminster to Bridgnorth road and 4 miles west of Stourbridge. Pubs, cafes, restaurants, Indian takeaway, chip shops, chemist, baker, groceries, bank, Post Office, phones, WC. Buses. Car parks off High Street.

Kinver Edge (SO 829822) (W33) (E320) - three armed signpost on ridge marks the meeting of three **LDPs,** the **North Worcestershire Path, Staffordshire Way** and **Worcestershire Way.** No road access or facilities.

(Pub) Bellman's Cross (Free House), Shatterford.

Arley (SO 765803) (W51) (304) - by River Severn
3.5 miles north of Bewdley and 2 miles west of A442
Kidderminster/Bridgnorth road. Pub, cafe, Post Office
& general store, phone. Steam trains on Severn Valley
Railway - 01299 401001. Car park. **Linked LDP -
Severn Way, Worcestershire Way.**

Cleobury Mortimer (SO 674758) (W78) (E275) - church
in centre of village on A4177 between Kidderminster
and Ludlow. Pubs, cafe, fish & chip shop, Chinese take
away, baker, general store, Post Office, phone. Buses,
street parking.

Hopton Wafers (SO 637766) (W88) (E265) - church in
hamlet on the A4177 between Cleobury Mortimer and
Ludlow. Pub, phone. Buses, no sensible parking.

Ludlow (SO 512742) (W131) (E227) - Ludford Bridge
on south side of town. All facilities including YHA.
Tourist Information - 01584 875053. Buses and trains.
Linked LDP - Shropshire Way, Mortimer Way.

Leintwardine (SO 402739) (W167) (E196) - bridge
over River Teme in village west of Ludlow on A4113.
Pubs, chip shop, Post Office, shop, garage, phone.
Buses, street parking.

Knighton (SO 288724) (W192) (E173) - town clock.
All facilities. Tourist Information - 01547 529424.
Buses, trains. Car park. **Linked LDPs - Llwbyr
Owain Glyndwr, Offa's Dyke Path.**

Llangunllo (SO 212713) (W208) (E159) - pub in small
village west of Knighton on B4356 north of A485. Pub
also housing community shop and Post Office, phone.
Buses and trains. **Linked LDP - Llwbyr Owain
Glyndwr.**

Llanddewi Ystradenni (SO 108686) (W236) (E129) - church in small village 11 miles west of Knighton on A483 Llandrindod Wells and Newtown road. Buses Pub closed, no facilities. Car space on roads.

Rhaeadr (SN 971680) (W276) (E91) - town clock. Pubs, tea shops, general store, banks, Post Office, phone, WCs. Tourist Information - 01597 810591. Buses. Car park. **Linked LDP - Wye Valley Walk.**

Llanerch (SN 901616) (W29) (EE78) - car park by bridge on road into the Claerwen Valley where stands a lonely phone box to call B&B that give lifts.

Ffair Rhos (SN 757681) (W299) (E71) - Ffair Rhos is a road junction on the B4343 1.5 miles west of this point on the route. Some buses. Pub & phone. You can call local B&Bs that give lifts and will return you next day.

Pontrhydygroes (SN 742727) (W310) (E61) - south side of road bridge over Afon Ystwyth in small village south of Devil's Bridge on B4343. Pub, Post Office & store. Buses -two per day. No nearby parking.

Pontarfynach/Devil's Bridge (SN 739769) (W324) (E49) - gate to railway station in village east of Aberystwyth on A4120. Hotel bar and tea rooms, shop & Post Office, phone. Buses, terminus of narrow gauge steam railway to Aberystwyth. **Linked LDP - Cambrian Way.**

Capel Seion (SN 632793) (W348) (E25) - end of lane by school in village east of Aberystwyth on B4120. Large chapel, graveyard, definitely no pub. Buses.

Aberystwyth (SN 583813) - north end of three arched stone bridge over Afon Rheidol. All facilities, Tourist Information - 01970 612125. Buses and trains.

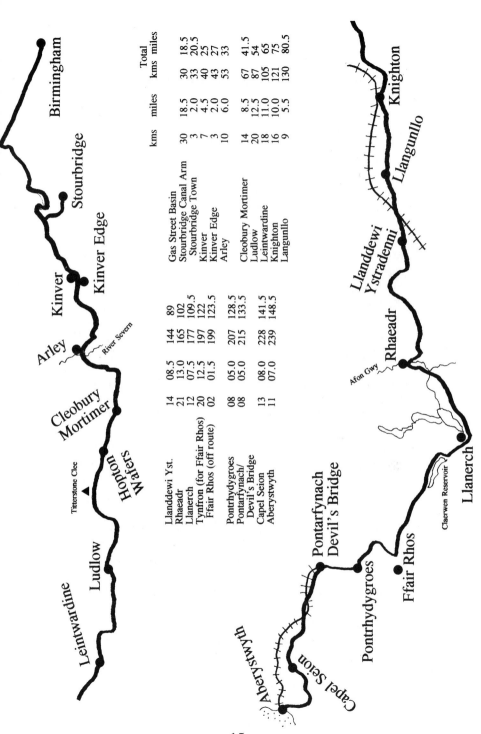

	kms	miles	Total kms	Total miles
Gas Street Basin				
Stourbridge Canal Arm	30	18.5	30	18.5
Stourbridge Town	3	2.0	33	20.5
Kinver	7	4.5	40	25
Kinver Edge	3	2.0	43	27
Arley	10	6.0	53	33
Cleobury Mortimer	14	8.5	67	41.5
Ludlow	20	12.5	87	54
Leintwardine	18	11.0	105	65
Knighton	16	10.0	121	75
Langunllo	9	5.5	130	80.5

Llanddewi Yst.	14	08.5	144	89
Rhaeadr	21	13.0	165	102
Llanerch	12	07.5	177	109.5
Tynfron (for Ffair Rhos)	20	12.5	197	122
Ffair Rhos (off route)	02	01.5	199	123.5
Pontrhydygroes	08	05.0	207	128.5
Pontarfynach/ Devil's Bridge	08	05.0	215	133.5
Capel Seion	13	08.0	228	141.5
Aberystwyth	11	07.0	239	148.5

Birmingham

Stourbridge

Kinver Edge

Kinver

Arley

River Severn

Cleobury Mortimer

Hopton Wafers

Titterstone Clee

Ludlow

Leintwardine

Pontarfynach Devil's Bridge

Pontrhydygroes

Ffair Rhos

Capel Seion

Aberystwyth

Llanerch

Claerwen Reservoir

Afon Gwy

Rhaeadr

Llanddewi Ystradenni

Langunllo

Knighton

Walk Stages & Accommodation

The general map shows the Starting Points with a table of distances so that you can work out your itinerary. Phone me on 01926 776363 for a free Accommodation List.

Distances between most Starting Points are well within the range of slower walkers, but there are two sections which might present some problems.

Birmingham to Stourbridge (Urban Section) 18.5 miles/ 30 kms. If you decide to walk this urban section you will not easily find accessible and low priced B&B, so it is best walked in one stage.

Rhaeadr to Pontrhydygroes (via Llanerch and Ffair Rhos) (25.5 miles/41 kms). This is a safe, all weather route with only one steep climb and experienced walkers will easily cover it in a day. However, if you want to break the walk be aware that **mobile phones do not work** over much of this area so you can't call a taxi. This is what to do:

Llanerch (7.5 miles/12 kms) has a phone box. The two B&B places listed below will collect you from this point and return you the next day. But YOU MUST book with them in advance.

Elan Valley Hotel, Nr Rhayader, Powys LD6 5HN. Tel/fax 01597 810 448, e mail: Hotel@elanvalley.demon. co.uk, website: http://www.rhayader.co.uk/elan

Colin & Jennie Francis, Ty-nant, Elan Valley, Nr Rhayader, Powys LD6 5HN. Tel 01597 811412.

Ffair Rhos (12.5 miles/20 kms). This is just a road junction 1.5 miles (2kms) off the route from Tynfron. There is a pub and a phone box. The B&Bs marked # on the Accommodation list will pick you up and return you the next day.

Starting/Finishing at Stourbridge

BY CAR.
From M5 Junction 4, take the A491. Stourbridge is sign-posted all the way. Otherwise, take the A456 Birmingham and Kidderminster road to Hagley and turn north. Once on the Stourbridge Ring Road whiz round till you find the bus and train station, which is off the outer side (left).

BY BUS.
Regular, frequent services run from Birmingham and nearby places to the bus station in Foster Street.

BY TRAIN.
Local trains run regularly from Birmingham to Stourbridge Junction. From the Junction catch the shuttle train to the Town station which is next to Foster Street bus station.

Starting from Stourbridge

(W1S) From bus station go under Ring Road & follow Foster St to High Street.

(W2S) Go R 300 yds to junction. Go ahead down Lower High St to bottom & take subway. Take next subway L into street.

(W3S) Go R 100yds, turn L on Canal Street & join canal towpath. Go 1.25 miles to main canal & cross footbridge.

WESTBOUND: Go L - next para (W26)

EASTBOUND: Go R - next para (E327)

Finishing at Stourbridge

(E1S) Cross bridge & take Stourbridge Arm for 1.25 miles to end of towpath. Go parallel with canal & join cobbled street to T junction.

(E2S) Go R 100 yds & take subway. Turn R to street & go ahead up to road junction. Go ahead 300 yds & take road L (Foster St).

(E3S) Take subway, turn R, then R again & up steps to bus station.

17

Merry Hill Marina, Dudley

Valley of River Redlake

Rhaeadr Falls

18

The
Birmingham &
Aberystwyth Walk

Starting Point	●
Path, with bridge	
Track	
Road/lane/drive	
Railway	
Canal	
Stream/river/lake	
Woodland	
Hedge/fence	
Church	+
Building	■
Pub	△

Maps are drawn to an approximate
scale of 2.5ins/1 mile - 4cms/1km
unless marked otherwise.

(W)

(W1) From Gas Street enter arch in 8ft brick wall & go L down ramp to face canal basin.

(W2) Go L (past pub & canal shop) & under tunnel. Go on 200 yds to canal junction by "nia"

(W3) Go L (Wolverhampton) & follow towpath 2.5 miles via:
- St Vincent St Bridge
- Monument Road Bridge
- start of Soho Loop R

- Lee Bridge
- Winson Green Bridge
- end of Soho Loop R
- 2 arch railway bridge
& flat concrete bridge to cast iron footbridge at canal junction.

(W4) Cross bridge & go L to cross next bridge. Bear L & go on with canal on your L 2.5 miles via:
- Rolfe Bridge
- gothic iron aqueduct
- flat steel bridge
- brick pump house
- concrete tunnel

- iron Galton Bridge
- 3 arch railway bridge
- brick & concrete bridge
- blue brick bridge
- stone bridge
& M5 bridge
to cast iron footbridge at canal junction. ▶▶▶

(E)

(E348) Cross iron foot-bridge & go R 1.5 miles via:
- M5 bridge
- stone bridge
- blue brick bridge
- brick & concrete bridge
- 3 arch railway bridge

- cast iron Galton Bridge
- concrete tunnel
- brick pump house
- brick arch bridge
- gothic iron aqueduct
& Rolfe Bridge to canal junction.

(E349) Cross iron foot-bridge & go R to cross next one. Go L 2.5 miles via:
- flat concrete bridge
- 2 arch railway bridge
- start of Soho Loop L

- Winson Green Bridge
- Lee Bridge
- end of Soho Loop L
- Monument Road Bridge
& St Vincent St Bridge
to canal juntion with island by "nia".

(E350) Follow same towpath & curve R. Go on 200 yds & under Broad Street Tunnel to

Birmingham

20

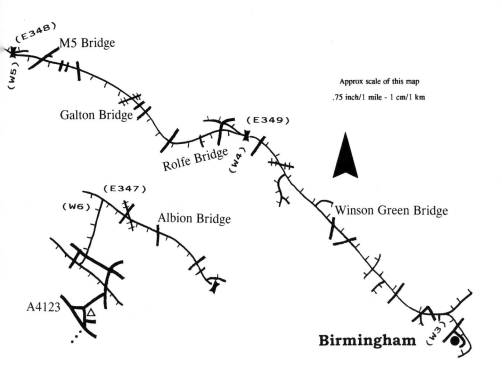

Approx scale of this map
.75 inch/1 mile - 1 cm/1 km

M5 Bridge (E348)
(W5)

Galton Bridge

Rolfe Bridge (E349)
(W4)

(E347)
(W6)   Albion Bridge

Winson Green Bridge

A4123

Birmingham (W3)

W

(W5) Cross bridge & go R
1.25 miles via:
- lattice footbridge
- Bromford Bridge
- Albion Bridge
- steel railway bridge
& iron & timber bridge
to canal junction.

(W6) Go L .5 mile (via 3
locks) to next canal. Go L
.4 mile to Brades Bridge
& take slope L to road.

(W7) Go R 150 yds & take
Brades Rise R. Go 350 yds
to T junction. Go L past
Prince of Wales & take
Bury Hill Rd to A4123.
►►►

E

(E345) Cross at traffic
lights & take Bury Hill
Road to its end. Bear L
past Prince of Wales &
take Brades Rise R for 350
yds to T junction.

(E346) Go L 150yds & cross
canal, then turn L onto
towpath. Go R (NOT under
Brades Bridge) for .4 mile
to canal junction.

(E347) Go R .5 mile via:
- iron & timber bridge
- steel railway bridge
- Albion Bridge
- Bromford Bridge
& lattice footbridge to
canal junction L. ◄

21

Gas Street Basin is where the Worcester & Birmingham Canal finishes its journey from the River Severn to meet the Birmingham Canal. The lock replaced a physical barrier which was in place for many years because the Birmingham Company refused to allow a junction. Now the gates stand permanently open and the levels of the two canals are the same, but the lock once gained the older Birmingham Company a small amount of water with each transit.

I first met the basin in the late 1960s when it was a secret and silent backwater, weedy, oily and dominated by great iron warehouses. In a raft of floating debris, decrepit narrowboats slumbered by the wharf piled with fuel logs, buckets of flowers and rusty bicycles. Now the tatty old boats have gone and the brickwork is neatly pointed. New cast iron bollards are smartly black and white, and a traditional pub kit has been brought from a traditional pub factory. It is all so impossibly clean.

The canals of Birmingham and the Black Country drift on in a dream world of their own, gliding past foundries, bakeries, warehouses, engineering shops, offices and transport yards. Engines hum, furnaces roar and heavy presses crash, but on the canals the water is still. Square, brick warehouses contemplate disused wharfs by stately iron bridges, and for most of the way the banks are green and flowering.

One hundred miles of waterways runs like veins though the body the West Midlands area, and this walk follows parts of four. From the start at Gas Street Basin it follows the **Birmingham Canal** which sweeps majestically through its cavernous cuttings to Wolverhampton. You are walking the 'New Main Line' built by Thomas Telford between 1826 and 1838, but its origins lie in 1768 when the Birmingham Canal Co employed the great canal pioneer, James Brindley, to construct their first waterway.

As with all the early canals, Brindley avoided changes of level by following the contours so as to minimise capital

spending on tunnels and large earthworks. The result
was the winding, rambling, heavily locked 'Old Main
Line'. It was a successful, profitable canal, but soon
became congested with traffic and slow. Telford's job
was to simplify and shorten the route. By 1825 the capital
market for raising money was much larger and profitable
experience of canals gave the courage to invest. Telford
cut his new canal on a straight line and avoided the need
for locks by digging the vast, green cuttings. The 'New
Main Line' absorbed part of Brindley's canal but cut off
several meanders, notably the Soho Loop, and you can
see the ends as branches off the main line. At Smethwick
Junction the two lines separate and run parallel courses.
I have taken you along Telford's Line. Brindley's quaint
curves certainly look more interesting to begin with, and
give a shorter walk, but there is one very nasty half mile
where it runs under the M5, satanically noisy, dark and
dirty. Look out for the gothic cast iron Engine Arm
Aqueduct and the lofty and graceful Galton Bridge.

Galton Bridge

Black Country scene

(W8) Cross at traffic lights & take steps on R of gates. Pass building, cross path & go ahead up rising grass path.

(W9) Pass trees on your R & keep this line past houses R, then go L by wire fence & cross iron stile.

(W10) Go ahead on grass path (towards masts) & cross 2nd stile, then on to 3rd stile & track.

(W11) CROSS TRACK & follow faint path uphill parallel with L hedge 150 yds, then go L through hedge gap. Go AHEAD & cross fence (or take gap) to road.

(W12) Go R a few paces, cross & take path through hedge gap into field corner. Follow L hedge & pass barrier onto road.

(W13) Cross & take stile. Go R on shale path 30 paces, then bear L to black & white post. Follow row of pines to yellow top post.

(W14) Turn sharp L & cross fairway to 2nd yellow top post, then go on to 3rd. Go R by pines down to orange sign, & cross stile onto drive. ▶▶

(E339) Go L, round R bend to next bend & cross stile R. Go ahead with trees on your L past black & white post to yellow top post.

(E340) Go L to 2nd yellow top post, then bear L across fairway to 3rd. Go R down line of pines to meet end of tarmac track. Go half L towards tower, & at orange sign cross stile onto lane.

(E341) Go ahead past barrier opposite into field. Follow R hedge to bottom corner, & take hedge gap to road.

(E342) Cross road, go R a few paces & cross fence by marked post. Go AHEAD midfield past R end of hedge. Go R down faint path to green track, & cross stile.

(E343) Follow R fence & cross 2nd stile. Go ahead on green path & cross 3rd stile.

(E344) Go half L by fence & follow path past houses. Keep same line down to A4123. ◀

24

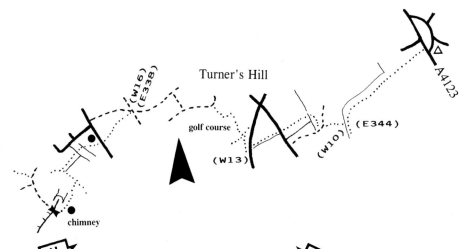

Turner's Hill

golf course

(W13)

chimney

(W15) Go L 150 yds & turn R down track to T junction. Go L down to end of L fence, plus 150 yds, to big holly bush R at path junction.

(W16) BEAR L on small RISING red shale path, & cross stile to B4171.

(W17) Cross road, go L 12 paces & cross stile R. Bear R on path to join fence, plus 12 paces, & take gap L. **SIGHT CHIMNEY** L ahead [brg 192], & find your own path to it.

(W18) Pass chimney etc on your L & cross canal bridge R. Follow gravel track 100 yds & take track R. Go 50 paces to R turn, then go AHEAD on grass path.

(E335) Go L past chimney & up green track ahead (not L) to stone path. Go L 100 yds UP TO L bend with information board.

(E336) Turn 90 deg R through bushes to field. Head for blue brick tower [brg 46] on green path, & take 2 fence gaps. Bear R past tower & cross stile to B4171.

(E337) Cross & take stile. Follow path curving R to path junction. Go ahead between bushes (past path R) & join fenced track.

(E338) Go up to end of R fence, then take track R up to tarmac drive.

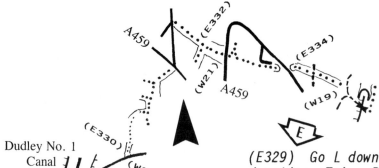

Dudley No. 1 Canal

Dudley No. 2 Canal

(W19) Follow with trees on your R & cross wide path. Go on via wooded cutting & nasty tunnel to join tarmac path.

(W20) Follow it past end of road R then with grass on L to end of bank, & take steps L down to road.

(W21) Cross & follow grass path to join fenced tarmac path, & go on to road. Go L to A459.

(W22) Cross & take gate opposite. Follow gravel path past falling path R & take steps. At fence corner pass path R & go 30 paces. Take next path R to gate & lane.

(W23) Go down R .3 mile (crossing canal) to road. Take road opposite 100 yds to steel gate R & join towpath. ►►

(E329) Go L down road to junction. Take Blackbrook Lane opposite & cross canal, then go 250 yds (past 1st gate L to 2nd) & take kissing gate L.

(E330) Follow path past R fork & steps L, then follow fence to its end. Go down L, then curve R up to gate & A459.

(E331) Cross & take New Road opposite. Pass last house R & factory gate, plus 75 yds to corner of factory fence, & take tarmac path R.

(E332) Pass works & when path bends sharp R, go ahead on grass path to road.

(E333) Cross, take steps up bank & turn R. Follow tarmac path past ends of roads & through nasty tunnel.

(E334) Take woodland path & cross a path. Keep this line 300 yds & pass 1st phone pole to 2nd. Take track L & cross canal. ◄

Turner's Hill with its masts and towers is a green public
space by which you can cross the watershed between the
Trent and Severn river systems. True, the northern flank is
scrubby in places, but it means that you have no significant
road walking between central Birmingham and Stourbridge.
On the summit you cross the greens of the Dudley Golf
Course to enter a Country Park lying across the southern
flank of the hill. On the eastern edge is a quarry which is
worked for dolerite, a dark igneous rock much in demand
for roadstone. The next outcrop of this rock is Titterstone
Clee which is similarly quarried.

The main landmark in the Park is **Cobb's Engine House**
with its iron-bound brick chimney. The engine in its now
roofless shed pumped water from local mines, but was sold
to the Henry Ford Museum at Dearborn, USA.

Next to the engine house is the southern portal of the 3,027
yard (1.7 miles/2.77 kms) **Netherton Tunnel** which links the
Birmingham New Main Line with the **Dudley No. 2 Canal**.
It was opened in 1858 as a relief for the narrow and sagging
Dudley Tunnel which runs parallel. If you like cold, dark
walks with occasional soakings from ventilation shafts, take
the towpath through the Netherton.

The Black Country Urban Forest is a gigantic planning
venture to plant two million trees in this hard worked
industrial area. Parks, schools, playing fields, car parks,
canals, roadsides and abandoned railway lines have been
planted, wherever there is space for trees. The result is
a healing green canopy which is soothing old scars.

After Turner's Hill, Cobb's Engine House and Baptist
End Nature Reserve, the walk joins the **Dudley No. 1
Canal**. This looping, winding canal with its many locks
was opened in 1779, and like all first generation canals
it hugs the contours and seems to explore the secret
corners of the Black Country.

The **Merry Hill Centre** comes as a visual shock. After the worn brick warehouses, rusty, dusty steel factories, 19th century cast iron bridges and quaint canal gear, you enter a green cutting. This curves round a bend and faces you with a clean, multiroofed, space age structure. You walk on past a gleaming marina with cafe bars, bistros, offices and a big hotel. It is all smart blue railings and fresh paint offset by a totally bogus traditional pub built in the 'brewers nostalgia' style.

As the canal whizzes across the flank of a hill you can observe the consumer ants far below in the monstrous shopping centre. Watch them park their little travelling machines and scurry into the hive to offer their tributes of nectar. Aren't we glad we're not consumer ants today? In the distance is the tower of Netherton church on top of its big, gorsey hill. This dense and teeming Black Country has so many strange, empty spaces.

Black Country warehouse

Cobb's Engine House

28

You will know the Redhouse Cone when you pass it and it shows that you are in Stourbridge glass country. It looks like a pottery kiln but actually housed a glass furnace, allowing heat to escape but protecting the glass blowers from the weather. It is now a small museum attached to Stuart Crystal, but nearby are several other firms famous for cut glass.

Shortly after the Cone, the canal leaves the urban area and follows the valley of the River Stour to meet the **Staffordshire & Worcestershire Canal**. Another early contour canal by Brindley, it was opened in 1772 to link the Trent & Mersey Canal near Stafford to the River Severn. Crockery and coal from the Potteries and Staffordshire coalfields rippled along at horse pace to Gloucester, Bristol and the west.

Stewpony Lock on the Staffs & Worcs Canal

(W24) Go L 3.7 miles via:
- Peartreelane Bridge
- iron footbridge
- Woodside Bridge
- deep steel bridge
- flat steel bridge

- Merry Hill Waterfront
- Green's Bridge
- Ninelocks Bridge
- iron footbridge
- concrete bridge

- striped bridge
- short steel bridge
- steel & brick bridge
- steel rail bridge
- Brettell Lane Bridge

- brick & steel bridge
- Brierley Bridge
- The Old Bush
- Farmer's Bridge
& Ley's Bridge to
pass feed canal R, cross
turnover bridge & go L.

(W25) Go ahead 1.25 mile
via:
- Brierley Hill Rd bridge
- Samson & Lion
- brick & concrete bridge
- small brick bridge
- brick cone L
- Glasshouse bridge
& brick bridge
to Stourbridge Arm of
canal L

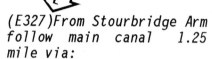

(E327) From Stourbridge Arm
follow main canal 1.25
mile via:
- small brick bridge
- Glasshouse Bridge
- glass cone
- small brick bridge

- brick & concrete bridge
- Samson & Lion
- Brierley Hill Rd Bridge
- 2 locks
plus 100 yds, & cross
turnover bridge L.

(E328) Follow canal for
3.7 miles via:

- Ley's Bridge
- Farmer's Bridge
- The Old Bush
- Brierley Bridge
- brick & steel bridge

- Brettell Lane Bridge
- steel railway bridge
- brick & steel bridge
- short steel bridge
- wire mesh bridge

- concrete bridge
- iron footbridge
- Ninelocks Bridge
- Greens Bridge
- Merry Hill Waterfront

- flat steel bridge
- deep steel bridge
- Woodside Bridge
- iron footbridge
& Peartreelane Bridge.
then turn R off canal onto
road.

30

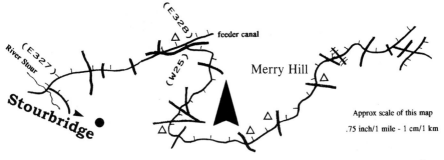

feeder canal

(E328)

(E327)

River Stour

(W25)

Merry Hill

Stourbridge

Approx scale of this map

.75 inch/1 mile - 1 cm/1 km

Stourbridge

Kinver

(W26) Go DOWNSTREAM 2.25 miles via:
- small brick bridge
- River Stour Aqueduct
- stepped parapet bridge
- small brick bridge
- brick bridge with pipe
- top lock
& concrete bridge (A449), to meet Staffs & Worcs Canal.

(W27) Cross brick bridge & go L 2 miles via:
- small brick bridge
- Stewpony New Bg (A458)
- Dunsley Tunnel
- Hyde Lock
 to bridge by Vine Inn, then go R onto road.

(W28) Go R into village up to Olde White Hart. ▶▶

(E324) Face Olde White Hart & go L .3 mile. Pass road R, go round L bend to to canal, & turn L onto towpath.

(E325) Follow 2 mile via:
- Hyde Lock
- Dunsley Tunnel
- Stewpony New Bdg (A458)
& small brick bridge to canal junction.

(E326) Cross Stourton Bridge & follow Stour-bridge Canal 2 mile via:
- top lock
- small brick bridge
- small brick bridge
- stepped parapet bridge
- River Stour Aqueduct
& small brick bridge to Stourbridge Arm R.

Kinver

Stourbridge ◀

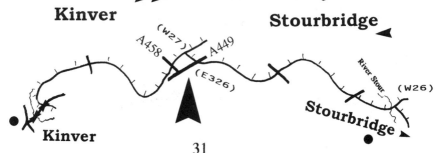

A458 (W27) A449

(E326)

River Stour

(W26)

Stourbridge ▶

Kinver

31

Kinver

(W29) Face Olde White Hart, go R & take Vicarage Drive L. At fork go R up to gates, then L down fenced path to road.

(W30) Go R 200 yds to junction by post box. Go L to 30mph sign & turn R up tarmac drive to its end.

(W31) Take path L of garage & take small gate. Go ahead 50 paces, turn R up steep, sandy path, then via wooden steps to grassy shoulder. Go L up to crest

(W32) Go L on ridge path 300 yds to where grassy spur veers L. Bear R past it & follow ridge .75 mile (past trig point) to 3 armed signpost.

Kinver Edge

(W33) From 3 armed signpost follow "Worcs Way" on main ridge path .5 mile. At high wire fence bear L to 2nd fence corner.

(W34) Go R through barrier to steel gates, then go L 100 yds to track junction.

►►

(E318) Cross & take rising path opposite, cross a path & reach wide track junction. Take wide green ride ahead up to fourway track junction.

(E319) Go L through barrier 175 yds to steel gates. Go R 50 yds to barrier. Go L by fence to join ridge track, & follow it .75 mile to 3 armed markpost.

Kinver Edge

(E320) From 3 armed markpost, take Staffs Way. Follow ridge path .9 mile, to its end at toposcope.

(E321)Go R down cliff edge path to grassy shoulder with markpost & wooden fence ahead. Go R down to crosspaths in hollow.

(E322) Go L & take small gate. Follow path, then drive (round R bend) to lane. Go L to junction by post box.

(E323) Go R 200 yds to "Church View" L, & just past it take path L. Go up to track, then go R & join lane to High Street.

Kinver

◄

(W35) Go R through barrier to pass seat L, & follow green track down to track junction. Go ahead on rising path 200 yds to road.

(W36) Take lane opposite 325 yds to R bend. Go ahead up track .3 mile to junction by house.

(W37) Go R up to bend & take stile/gate ahead. Cross top of field & take stile/gate onto earth track.

(W38) Follow 1 mile to junction with hard track.

➤

(E316) Turn sharp R & follow track 1 mile, till it bends L by pond to meet gates.

(E317) Take stile ahead, cross top of field & take stile/gate onto track. Go ahead to junction & turn L. Go .3 mile to bend of lane. Go ahead to road.

◄

Kinver

(E323)

(W30)

(E321)

(W32)

Kinver Edge

(W34)

(E318)

(W36)

Start's Green

(E317)

Castle Hill Farm

(W37)

33

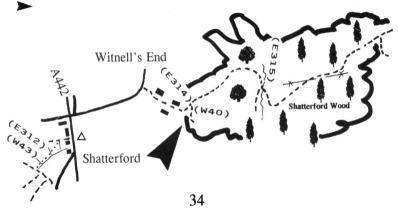

(W39) Go L .6 mile (past name board & power lines, track falls and curves L, then R) to SHARP L bend over stream.

(W40) Go R down to cross stream, then L .3 mile to meet bend of hard track.

(W41) Bear R, pass build-ings & go 300 yds to bend of lane. Go L .3 mile to A442.

(W42) Go L 200yds to pub. Pass under its arch, plus 100 yds to steel gate, & cross stile. Bear L over paddock & pass pond close on your L. Go through grove of trees, then follow L fence to field corner & cross stile.

(W43) Follow L fence to field corner & cross stile onto track. Go up L to join stone track. Go up 25 yds & turn R on green track.

(E311) Go L 25 yds, then take earth track on R for 25yds & cross stile R. Follow R fence & cross corner stile to field.

(E312) Follow R fence to near pond, then bear L to pass it on your R (through trees) into open paddock. Head just L of red brick shed & cross stile onto track. Go on to A442.

(E313) Go L 200yds to cross -roads. Go R .3 mile to L bend & take stone track R. Go between buildings & round L bend to reach sharp R bend.

(E314) Go ahead past big post & follow wooded track down .3 mile, to cross stream & reach hard track.

(E315) Go L .6 mile (past forest name board & green gate) to see cypress hedge R by white gate. DON'T GO THROUGH.

Witnell's End

A442

Shatterford

(E312)
(W43)

(E314)

(W40)

(E315)

Shatterford Wood

Kinver is a sprawling village, but confined by the bulk of Kinver Edge to the south and the River Stour and the Staffs & Worcs Canal curling round to the east, it still has a focus in its High Street. This is a pleasing assortment of timber framed and brick buildings. The village first grew up close to St Peter's church, high on a sandstone hill above the flood plain of the Stour. There had been wool, but after its decline came flax making, hatting, gloving and the iron trade. The river powered the village's industrial revolution in the 19th century, and at one time there were five iron mills around the village. Kinver Mill by the canal lock was powered by three waterwheels to make iron and steel wire.

Kinver Edge is a glorious great sandstone whale of a hill some two miles long which reaches a height of 166 metres. Its caves, hollows and acres of woodland are owned partly by the National Trust and partly by Worcestershire County Council. From the summit are misty views of the Clent Hills, The Sheepwalks, the Clee Hills, Abberley Hills and Malverns. The Edge lies roughly north to south with the western side steep and abrupt and the eastern flank a broad and gentle slope into the valley of the River Stour. Most of the trees forming the dense canopy over the edge are birch, but there is a good spread of sessile oak, all self seeding healthily, with plantations of Scots pine, Corsican pine and larch.

The ramparts of an **Iron Age hill fort** can be seen some 200 yards south of the summit toposcope. They enclosed only 7.5 acres, small as such enclosures go, and can only have served as an emergency retreat.

Cave dwellings carved out of the rosy sandstone at Holy Austin Rock on the northern tip of the Edge were occupied in the Middle Ages by hermits. During the early 1900s twelve families lived in the houses which were later fitted with gas and a piped water supply, and some houses were still inhabited in the 1950s.

(W44) Follow to T junction. Go up L between gateways to T junction.

(W45) Go R past 1st & 2nd timber houses & take gate into wood. Go L .3 mile (via dip where track R joins), then cross rise & dip, up to track junction with Worcs Way post.

(W46) Go ahead on main earth track to track junction. Go ahead on hard track .4 mile (down to cross low bridge & up) to next track junction.

(W47) Go ahead on EARTH track past posts & side path L, plus 75 yds, to fork. Go R & down to meet hard track by low bridge. Go L over bridge to track junction.

(W48) Go R (past track R) up to steel gates, & cross stile R. Go L past house & take corner gate.

▶

(E306) Go ahead past house & bear R to cross stile onto track. Go L 250yds to crosstracks by steel tank.

(E307) Go L on hard track, cross low bridge & take green track R. Follow for .3 mile (join rising path from R & pass 2 posts) up to track junction.

(E308) Go ahead on hard track .4 mile (across low bridge) to junction where hard track turns R. Go ahead on earth track 350 yds to next junction. (Worcs Way turns L)

(E309) Go ahead (curve R & down to cross dip, then rise & cross 2nd dip) to fork. Go R 175 yds (track from L joins) & take gate R.

(E310) Go ahead past 2 timber houses & through gateway in wooden fence. Go L on track (past white house) & take next track R to stone track.

◀

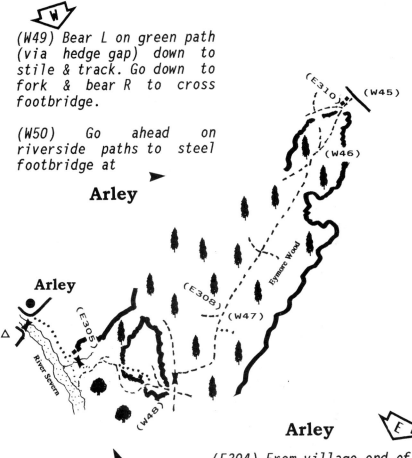

W

(W49) Bear L on green path (via hedge gap) down to stile & track. Go down to fork & bear R to cross footbridge.

(W50) Go ahead on riverside paths to steel footbridge at

Arley

Arley

(E310) (W45)

(W46)

Eymore Wood

(E308) (W47)

(E305)

River Severn

(W48)

Arley **E**

(E304) From village end of footbridge, go DOWNSTREAM on riverside paths .3 mile to cottage, & cross foot-bridge.

(E305) Go L & up to meet track. Go up (past L fork) to R bend, & cross stile into field. Follow grass path (via hedge gap) to house & take small gate.

Three **Long Distance Paths** meet on Kinver Edge.
The southern tip of the Staffordshire Way completes its
95 mile journey from Congleton Edge in Cheshire, the
48 mile Worcestershire Way starts its run south to the
Malvern Hills, while the North Worcestershire Path
sets off east on a 27 mile tour of Country Parks and
wonderful scenery to end at an anonymous point on the
Solihull boundary. To give the Path a proper destination
I extended it with the Midland Link. This 20 mile walk
through Warwickshire crosses the Heart of England Way
and ends in Kenilworth at Warwickshire's Centenary Way.
The Birmingham & Aberystwyth Walk adds a fourth LDP.

The walk crosses two small ridges before starting the long
descent to the River Severn through **Eymore Wood**. Though
planted mainly with Norway spruce and some stands of larch,
cyprus and Scots pine, the edges are softened by oak, self
seeded birch, hazel and holly, with a little beech. There
are also a few very large poplars and sweet chestnut trees.

Arley, strictly Upper Arley, was a little port on the
Severn. For a period from 1727 the river was navigable
as far upstream as Welshpool, but the lower reaches were
a vital transport artery from the earliest times. This is
illustrated by the age of St Peter's sandstone church
which overlooks the village. Although Victorianised
in a restoration of 1885, the nave and tower date from
1135 and other parts from the 14th and 15th centuries.

A **ferry** crossed the river from the 13th century, docking
at the slipways on either bank, until 1971 when the last
ferryman retired. It was replaced by the efficient but
charmless tubular steel footbridge.

Arley Station on the Severn Valley Railway has been
restored in the Great Western style of between the two
World Wars. It has won awards for Best Kept Station
and been used as a film set. The line carries steam trains
for the 16 miles between Kidderminster and Bridgnorth.

Opened in 1862 between Hartlebury, near Droitwich, to Shrewsbury, it carried mainly agricultural traffic and coal from the mines at Highley. Dr Beeching's notorious axe closed the line in 1963 and track north of Bridgnorth was lifted. The story of the present SVR started in 1965 when the preservation society was formed. The line was bought in stages as money could be raised, and after colossal efforts by volunteer workers the line was reopened from Bridgnorth to Bewdley in 1974. The section from Bewdley to Kidderminster, the vital link to main line services, was opened in 1984. The SVR runs regular services throughout the year and offers many special services, such as Santa Specials at Christmas, proper dining cars and marriage ceremonies.

The Author in his Kinver rock house

Nostalgia at Arley Station

(W51) From village side of river, cross bridge to road. Go .4 mile (past station, track R & 1st track L) to take 2nd track L.

(W52) Pass pond & gateway, then turn R into field. Head past midfield oak [brg 186] to top R field corner, & cross stile.

(W53) Bear L to top field corner & cross stile onto track. Go R 400 yds to bend of road.

(W54) Go R 30 paces to gate L, & cross stile. Go to far R field corner & cross stile. Go ahead, then with garden fence on your R, to bend of track.

(W55) Cross track & take green path to stone shed. Go L & take 1st path L to track. Go L to L bend, then take path R & cross stile into forest.

(W56) Go 150 yds to crosspaths. Go L, IGNORE stile L & follow wood edge path past house to B4194.

(W57) Go L past pub to end of wall & cross stile R. Follow R hedge to gate & cross stile.

▶

(E298) Pass house & follow wood edge path (past Woodland Trust gate) to crosspaths with stile R. DON'T CROSS IT. Follow path opposite to crosspaths. Go R 150 yds to cross stile & reach track.

(E299) Go L past "Cherry Trees" to end of garden hedge, & take path R. Join path from L & go on to stone shed. Go R to bend of track by house.

(E300) Go with garden fence on your L to its corner, then keep ahead & cross stile into field. Go ahead to gate & cross stile onto road.

(E301) Go R 30 paces to bend & take paved track L. Go 400 yds past house, sheds & woodland, to cross stile L

(E302) Go half R & cross midfence stile. Go half L [brg 6] past midfield oak & down to bottom R field corner. Exit onto track & go L to lane.

(E303) Go R .4 mile past station & cross river to

Arley

◀

40

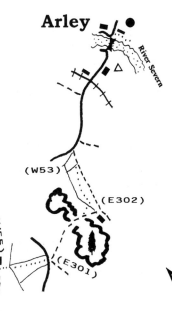

Arley

River Severn

(W53)

(E302)

(E301)

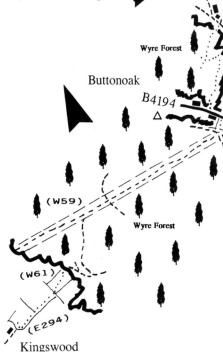

Wyre Forest

Buttonoak

B4194

(W59)

Wyre Forest

(W61)

(E294)

Kingswood

(W58) Go ahead up grass ride .5 mile to crest. Go ahead 150 yds & take track L.

(W59) Go down .3 mile (past conservation sign L) to T junction of tracks.

(W60) Go R & down (past rising track R) to cross fence & stream.

(W61) Go to top L field corner & cross stile. Follow wooded track (via gate & past ruin) to field top, & take gate.

(E293) Go R & follow field edge track down to take gate. Go on down wooded track to stile & field.

(E294) Go to bottom L field corner to cross stream & fence. Go up track to pass track from L, plus 85 paces to T junction of tracks.

(E295) Go up L .3 mile to wide grass ride.

(E296) Go R .5 mile (over crest & down to bottom gates) to cross stile.

(E297) Follow L fence & cross stile onto B4194. Go L 100 yds (past pub) to power pole, then cross road into gravel entrance.

You first meet the **Wyre Forest** at the bracken and gorse clad clearing of Pound Green Common. It was noted in the Domesday Book and experts say that its general shape and extent may not have changed significantly since. Nearby is Buttonoak. The name may be a corruption of 'boothen' a wigwam shelter where charcoal burners lived whilst their mounds were burning. The other industries of the area were basket and besom making and tree barking for the tanning trade at Bewdley. The Forest now covers some 6,000 acres between the Severn and Cleobury Mortimer. However, we should count some outlying woods to the north, valleyside woods to the south and the tongue of woodland east of the river reaching towards Kinver, for all of them were once part of the mediaeval forest.

The walk through the Forest is a series of climbs and falls to cross the valleys of three parallel brooks running roughly north to south into the Dowles Brook and the River Severn. For a commercial forest the Wyre has a high proportion of oak and some beech. This route passes largely through Norway spruce, but there is still variety and interest in odd clearings and especially by the streams, where you will find birch, oak and hazel.

After the pub at Buttonoak the walk follows a broad, grassy ride which is the course of the **Elan Valley Aqueduct**. This vast scheme opened in 1904 to bring fresh, moorland water from mid Wales to Birmingham, parts of Shropshire and the Black Country. From the Elan and Claerwen Reservoirs, which you meet much later in the walk, the water runs its 70 mile journey by gravity. In places it is very dramatic, plunging down steep valleys and shooting up mighty hills to reach the reservoirs at Frankley and Bartley Green on the southern edge of Birmingham. This broad ride is a good example. Look out for the blocky brick thingys with lots of locked hatches and a curiously funereal line in iron railings.

Winter in the Wyre

Taking the waters at Arley

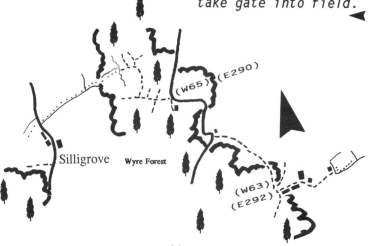W

(W62) Pass house & join hard track for .3 mile (past houses) to track junction on forest corner.

(W63) Go R (past track R a few paces on) for .4 mile to road.

(W64) Go R .3 mile (via L bend) to sharp R bend, & take SMALL gate ahead.

(W65) Go 100 yds (past 2 tracks R) to fork, & take track R. Go 200 yds & pass track R, plus 25 yds, to fork. Go ahead & down to cross two streams.

(W66) Go parallel with stream R (past iron gate L) & up to cross stile into field. Follow L hedge (via stile) to lane.

E

(E287) Go R into field, follow R hedge (via stile) & cross stile into woodland.

(E288) Go ahead parallel with stream L (past iron gate R) & down to cross 2 streams.

(E289) Go up ahead to join track from L. Pass track L & curve R 200 yds to T junction. Go L up to SMALL gate & road.

(E290) Go ahead .3 mile (round R bend) to brick shed, & take track L.

(E291) Go .4 mile to track junction on forest corner, pass 1st track L & take 2nd past bungalow.

(E292) Go 400 yds to 3 gates, then jink L & take earth track. Pass house & take gate into field.

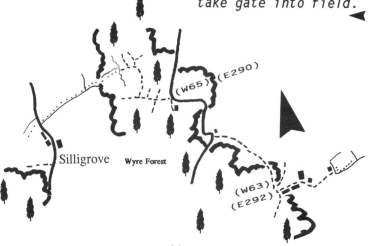

Silligrove   Wyre Forest

(W65) (E290)

(W63) (E292)

****
TEMPORARY ROUTE

Work is in hand to remove
obstructions on the Right
of Way. Phone 01926 776363
to check the present
position, and possibly get
new directions.

(W67T) Go L 400 yds (past
farm) & take fishery gate
R.

(W68T) Go 150 yds & take
stile L onto broad grass
ride. Go .5 mile (crossing
track) & cross stream by
pipes.

(W69T) Go up 150 yds to
hard track. Go L 200yds to
junction.

(W70T) Go R .5 mile (via
sharp bends, past pond &
then up) to junction with
earth track R. Go R to
forest edge.

END OF DIVERSION, MAIN

ROUTE RESUMES ▶

****

****

TEMPORARY ROUTE

Work is in hand to remove
obstructions from the
Right of Way. Phone 01926
776363 to check the
present position, and with
luck, get fresh directions

(E284T) Follow earth track
to meet hard track. Go L
.5 mile (past pond &
round sharp bends) to
track junction.

(E285T) Go L to wide grass
ride. Go R .6 mile (across
valley & through gate) to
end of ride, & cross stile
onto track.

(E286T) Go R & take gate
to lane. Go L 400yds (past
farm R) to phone pole with
stile L. DON'T CROSS IT.

DIVERSION ENDS

MAIN ROUTE RESUMES ◀

****

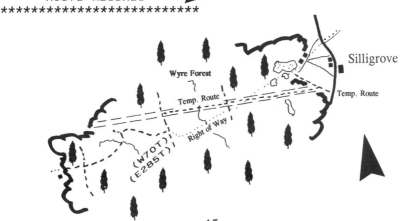

W

(W71) Take gate & go ahead with trees on your L. Join tarmac path to golf club.

(W72) Go ahead on tarmac drive, pass drive L plus 140 paces, & take path R. At gate go L on wood edge path to stile & B4201.

(W73) Go R 100 yds (past track L) & take gap L. Go half L across track to far hedge, & take small gate.

(W74) Go R & follow R hedge .4 mile to 10 yds from fence at field end. Take path R through bushes to A4177.

(W75) Go R on verge, cross side road & take stile R. Go parallel with river, heading for L end of houses, & cross stile onto drive.

(W76) Go ahead & take gate. Go half L & take small gate to cross foot-bridge. Follow L hedge up (via small gate) to road.

(W77) Go ahead to A4177 & turn R into village.

Cleobury Mortimer

E

(E276) Take kissing gate, follow R hedge & cross footbridge. Take kissing gate & go R (via gate) onto drive.

(E277) Cross stile ahead, go parallel with river, & take steps & stile up to A4177.

(E278) Go L, cross side road & follow verge 25 yds to cross stile L. Bash through bushes into field.

(E279) Go up L by hedge .4 mile, & take small gate L. Cross to field corner & take hedge gap onto B4201.

(E280) Go R 100 yds & cross stile L.

(E281) Follow hedged path (across tarmac path & past gate L) to meet drive.

(E282) Go L past cottage drive to golf club.

(E283) Pass buildings on your R & join tarmac path. Pass octagonal shelter to sharp L bend. Keep ahead with trees on your R & take gate into forest. ◄

Cleobury Mortimer

(E275) Stand in main road facing church, go R 325 yds & take New Road L. Go 200 yds & take steep tarmac path L.

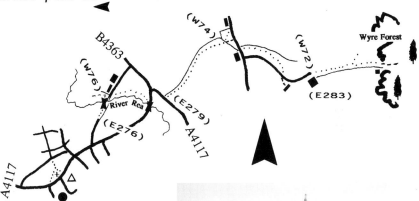

Cleobury Mortimer

Cleobury Mortimer

River Rea

47

Cleobury
Mortimer

(W78) Go to upper corner
of churchyard. Take tarmac
path to road & continue on
path opposite to join
road. Go ahead to cross-
roads.

(W79) Go L to L bend &
enter field. Pass R side
of social club & child
cages, & go L to hedge
corner. Go R & cross stile

(W80) Bear R to just L of
line of trees & take gate.
Bear R to top field corner
& take gate onto lane.

(W81) Cross stile opposite
heading for red brick
house, & join track.

(W82) Curve R past stone
house & take gate L. Go
ahead to field corner &
cross stile. Follow L
hedge & take gate. Go
ahead to R side of mound &
take gate onto lane.

(W83) Go R a few paces &
take gate opposite. Bear
R heading for L end of
poplars [brg 314] & cross
stile. Go ahead to L end
of conifers & take 2 gates

►

(E269) Go up to R end of
poplars & cross stile. Go
diagonally between fences
[brg 133] to lone skyline
treetop, then (when in
view) head just L of
reservoir mound, & take
gate onto road.

(E270) Go R a few paces &
take gate opposite. Follow
power poles to hedge &
take gate. Follow R hedge
& cross stile to orchard.

(E271) Head for far end of
grey barn & take gate
onto track. Go R & round L
bend, then step R into
field corner.

(E272) Go half L past
midfield oak to bog brush
tree, & cross stile onto
lane.

(E273) Take gate opposite.
Head for distant mast [brg
115] & R end of bottom
trees, to take gate. Head
for mast & cross stile.

(E274) Go to end of hedge,
go L past child cages,
then R past building to
road. Go ahead to
crossroads. Go R to end of
road & join tarmac path to

Cleobury
Mortimer ◄

(W84) Go half L to join R fence & follow it to field corner. Go through wide gap into next field, keep ahead to field corner & take gate onto track.

(W85) Cross stile L, go parallel with R fence & take gate. Go half R to bottom R field corner & take gate.

(W86) Pass pond & cross stile L. Go R past stone shed, take small gate & go ahead to stile & road.

(W87) Take road ahead .5 mile down to church at

Hopton Wafers

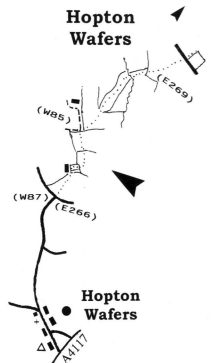

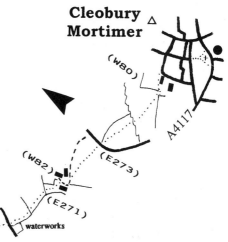

Cleobury Mortimer

Hopton Wafers

(E265) Put your back to church gate & go L .5 mile to T junction.

(E266) Cross stile opposite, head to R side of buildings & take small gate. Go ahead & cross stile. Go R past pond & take gate.

(E267) Curve L to pass humps on your L, then go parallel with L hedge (via gate) to stile & track.

(E268) Go R through gate. Go half L & through gap between end of hedge R & wire fence L. Follow L fence, bearing R to take 2 steel gates.

Cleobury Mortimer's rising, curving main street is an harmonious huddle of buildings. Some of the grander ones were built in a soft, local sandstone but most of the facades are of 18th century brickwork. However, some of the brick may conceal timber framed structures of the 16th and 17th centuries. As transport systems improved and brick became more cheaply available, a durable brick cladding became practicable and fashionable. Most of the visible timber work is Victorian, and correspondingly showy.

Peering drunkenly over the village is the twisted spire of the church of St Mary the Virgin. It has a 14th century timber frame, possibly unique, which seems to have contorted itself after the warping of wooden shingles fitted in a restoration of 1898. The earliest visible parts of the church are in the lowest part of the tower, and they are Norman, but there are many features from the 13th century. The interior of the church is large and lofty and rather gloomy, but it has a most attractive floor of Victorian encaustic tiles. Get the interesting booklet.

Cleobury has two **literary connections**. William Langland who wrote *The Vision of Piers Plowman* was born here in 1332. His great book is illustrated in the east window of St Mary's. Simon Evans was the local postman from 1928 to 1940 when he died aged 45. His essays appeared in the *Birmingham Post* and the *Post Office Magazine* and his talks were broadcast by the BBC. Simon Evans wrote about his thoughts and feelings, about his postman's round of 20 miles on foot and about nature and this Shropshire countryside.

The **Elan Valley** scheme shows itself again on the high ground to the west of Cleobury. Some 400 yards south of the hill top reservoir which supplies local needs is a stately little building. Its function may be mysterious but the architecture is delightful. Built in rosy red brick with sandstone quoins and dressings, there is an imposing pediment over the door and a low parapet of ornamental ironwork.

Hopton Wafers in the valley of the Mill Brook is pretty unremarkable apart from its name. The Wafer bit seems to have come from a Norman family, de Wafre, who were granted the land shortly after William the Conqueror's bit of nationalization. The church of St Michael was built in 1827 in 'sort of' classical style but some windows were later made more mediaeval looking. The churchyard sets it off nicely and has one whacking great tomb, which seems rather unsettled.

Hopton Manor is the big brick house opposite the church. **Hopton Court** is quite out of sight down its curving drive, so it is no use telling you that it has a verandah along the ground floor supported by unfluted Ionic columns, nor that it was built by John Nash. And you probabably don't care that the grounds were laid out by Humphrey Repton.

An iron kissing gate in the churchyard brings you directly onto rising fields and a rapid change in the landscape. A couple of fields up from the village and the character of the country starts to become wilder and tougher. The fields are now rough grazing with swathes of reeds and bracken and the hedges grow wild. Quite suddenly you cross a cattle grid to reach open moorland.

Mysterious water thingy

51

Hopton Wafers

(W88) Enter church gate, head for porch but go L on grass path & take iron gate. Go ahead through hedge & cross stile. Bear L to stream, take gate L & cross stile into field.

(W89) Go R by stream, pass 2 big oaks to cross plank bridge R, & take gate. Follow hollow & take gate onto track.

(W90) Cross track & go ahead (past gate R) & through gateway. Keep parallel with stream & take next gate. Head 25yds L of stream & cross fence, plank & 2 stiles, into bracken field.

(W91) Go ahead to top of field & take midhedge gate. Bear L & take mid-fence gate. Go half R to gap in holly hedge. Cross stile to field corner with fence on your R (not L).

(W92) Head for L side of building, take gate & follow track to road.

(E260) Go 150 yds past 1s track L & take 2nd (T glass). Pass 1st house curve R past 2nd & tal gate by stable.

(E261) Go L, follow hedge to field corner cross stile (bust?). (half R & take midfenc gate. Bear L to far er of field, & take midfenc gate into bracken field.

(E262) Go parallel with fence/stream to bottom c field, & cross 2 stiles plank & fence. Go ahea via gate, then gateway, go down to cross a track take steel gate

(E263) Go ahead dow hollow & take gate. Cros plank bridge & go L b stream 200yds, to cros stile L.

(E264) Take gate, go R cross stile. Head fo church (via hedge gap) take iron kissing gate t churchyard, & exit to roa

Hopton Wafers

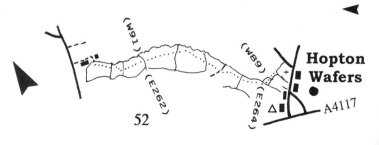

Hopton
Wafers

A4117

52

The **Clee Hills** were always harsh and inhospitable but an Iron Age camp covering 71 acres once occupied the top of Titterstone. Later the scars and waste left by quarrying for coal, iron, dolerite and copper since at least 1235 have made Titterstone Clee old and ugly. The modern quarries extract roadstone, much as the one on Turner's Hill in the Black Country. To the north and over Brown Clee, the moorland is exciting and invites walking, but Titterstone is all tailings and tips and strange little ponds. There are reeds, coarse grass, gorse, scratchy little farms and rusty, barbed wire fences. The ground around the quarries is mean and grey. In complete and happy contrast, the views are breathtaking.

Rising from Hoptonbank where you enter the moorland, there are **views** to the east of Kinver Edge, the Clent Hills and Wychbury Hill with its finger like obelisk. To the south are the Abberley Hills, with the huge clock tower at Great Witley, and the Malverns. From the centre of the moorland you can see far to the north, with Brown Clee, Wenlock Edge and the Long Mynd. And as you cross to the western edge there are range upon range of magical hills - the Black Mountains and Hay Bluff, Bringewood Chase and High Vignols, the Clun and Radnor Forests. Titterstone Clee reaches 533 metres but this walk only crosses its shoulder at about 450 metres.

On Titterstone you meet the **Shropshire Way,** a 125 mile circular tour of the county with its southern tip at Ludlow and the northern end at Wem. There are spurs to the north and west which make a total of 172 miles. The Birmingham & Aberystwyth Walk shares footpaths with the Shropshire Way for the first and last miles of the long descent towards Ludlow and the River Teme.

The walk continues by picking a route through an intense tangle of interweaving footpaths, suggesting that in the past the area had a considerable population coming and going about its business.

W

(W93) Go R, cross cattle grid plus 30yds, & turn L onto side road.

****

OPEN COUNTRY

The route described below follows this road, then a rough track, see sketch map. You can go straight across the common on bearing 277 to meet the track at its junction with a quarry track.
****

(W94) Go 300 yds & turn L. Follow stone track .6 mile (past quarry track L & round R bend) to gate of house.

(W95) Go L 70 paces to where hard track turns L through gate. Go ahead up earth track & bend L, then go on 15 paces to bend R.

(W96) Rise on green track parallel with fence & trees R, then swing L for 350 yds (past ponds R) to join track from L.

(W97) Go ahead 350 yds & join hard track from R. Go 300 yds & pass fenced area R, then curve L 50 yds to track junction.

E

(E256) Tracks bear L & R. Bear R up to crest of ridge [brg 139]. At fork take grass track L to dead tree by small pond [brg 90]. Continue on grass track [brg 104] to junction of hard tracks.

(E257) Go L on hard track 300 yds till it bends L. Go ahead on green track 350yds to fork. Go L past ponds & curve L towards fence, then go parallel with it to join hard track by gate L. DON'T TAKE IT.

(E258) Go ahead past house L & round bend to quarry track R. DON'T TAKE IT.

****

OPEN COUNTRY

The route described below follows the main track to a road leading off the common, see sketch map. If you like this sort of thing you can go directly across the moor on brg 96 to the cattle grid.
****

(E259) Follow track .5 mile to road. Go R 300 yds to road junction. Go R & cross cattle grid.

54

(W98) Take grass track to dead tree by small pond [brg 284]. Pass them on your R & follow track to low crest [brg 270].

(W99) Follow track (now rutted) which bears R [brg 318] & meets lane near a road junction. ►

Titterstone Clee

(W95)
(E258)
(W97)
(W98)
(E257)
(E256)
(W99)

St Michael's, Hopton Wafers

55

(W100) Go R & take side lane L. Pass 2 quarry tracks R, round bends & go down to near side of house

(W101) Go L by wall on green track. Cross foot-bridge & curve up R to take small gate. Go to far top field corner, & cross stile.

(W102) Go half L with power poles to far top field corner, & cross stile. Get clear of gorse but follow L fence to field corner, cross stream & take gate.

(W103) Go R & cross midfence stile. Head for L side of buildings & take steel gate, then more gates, to pass house R & enter field.

(W104) Follow R fence to corner & cross (bust?) stile ahead into garden. Go ahead via stiles into field. Go half R & take gate. Go to far R field corner & cross stile.

►

(E251) Bear R & take gate. Bear R & cross stile onto drive. Cross low stile & garden to (bust?) corner stile & field.

(E252) Follow L fence & take gate. Go ahead through farm to field. Go ahead & cross midfence stile. Bear L to far bottom field corner & take gate.

(E253) Cross stream, bear L to clear gorse but follow R fence to field corner & cross stile. Follow power poles (past heap of stones) to R of last pole, & cross stile.

(E254) Follow R hedge to corner, then L past white house to corner, & take small gate. Go down, cross footbridge & curve up L to hard track.

(E255) Go up R .3 mile to road. Go R 125 yds & cross stream to markpost & grass tracks L. ◄

(E249) Go L a few paces &
take lane opposite. Go .3
mile to wooded green track
R with gate either side.

(E250) Correct route runs
up track 75 yds, then L
over stile into field
corner.

IF OBSTRUCTED take L of 2
gates, follow R hedge &
take gateway into next
field.

Cross field diagonally
(through gappy hedge) to
top field corner, & cross
stile in L fence.

(W105) Go half R through
gappy hedge to far bottom
field corner, & cross
fence onto track. Go R to
lane.

IF OBSTRUCTED: Go through
gateway & follow L hedge
to gate & lane.

(W106) Go L .3 mile to
A4117.

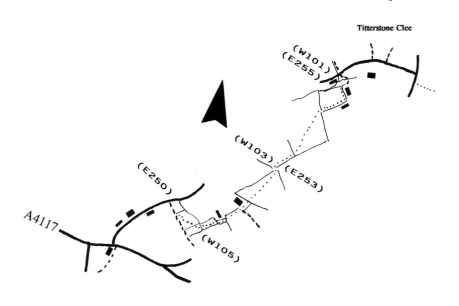

Titterstone Clee

(W107) Go L a few paces &
take track opposite to T
junction of tracks. Take
green track opposite/R,
pass house & go down to
road.

(W108) Take gate L (No. 11
Hawthorn), pass house &
take gate/stile. Follow
hollow track up 150 yds &
cross stile R.

(W109) Go L & cross stile.
Go ahead (via green shed &
hedge gap) & cross stile
into field.

(W110) Go ahead across
summit & (when in view)
head for R side of churchyard & cross stile. Follow
fenced path to car park &
road.
▶

(E245) Go R up hedge (via
gate) to steel gate &
road. Cross into car park
& take stile by church-
yard gate.

(E246) Follow fenced path
& cross stile into field.
Go ahead across summit &
down to cross stile.

(E247)Go ahead (via shed &
hedge gap) & cross stile.
Go R & cross stile. Go L
(via gate) & take gate
onto drive with road L.

(E248) Go R up tarmac
drive, pass L of garage &
follow earth track to
stone track. Take track
opposite/R to A4117. ◀

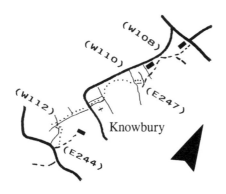

58

(W111) Take gate opposite, follow L hedge down via 1st gate to 2nd, & cross stile L.

(W112) Follow R hedge 60 paces & cross stile R. *[Barbed wire is unhookable]* Follow R hedge past its corner, then go ahead to outer gate & cross stile onto lane.

(W113) Go L 100 yds to house & take track R. Go 300 yds (past track L) & take gate into field.

(W114) Follow L hedge to field corner with 2 gates. Take L gate, follow L hedge to corner & take gate.

(W115) Go R by hedge through 2 gates. Follow L hedge (via 1 gate) to next field corner with gateway L, & cross stile ahead.

(W116) Pass brick thingy on your L, then head for far bottom field corner, & cross stile onto drive.

(E240) Cross bridge & cross stile L. Follow L hedge to near wooden gate L. Go R & pass brick thingy close on your L to field corner, & cross stile between 2 trees.

(E241) Pass gateway R & follow R hedge through 1st gate & up to take 2nd. Follow L hedge through 1st gate to field corner with 2 gates.

(E242) Take L gate, follow R hedge & take gate. Go R by R hedge to house, & take gate onto track.

(E243) Go ahead up to road, go L 100 yds to gate & cross stile on its L.

(E244) Go half L to projecting hedge corner, then with hedge on your L up to cross stile. *[Barbed wire is unhookable.]* Go L up hedge & cross corner stile.

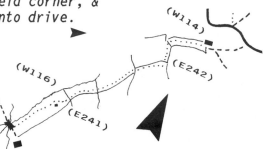

59

The long descent towards Ludlow is interrupted by a fine
feature, **Caynham Camp**, an Iron Age earthwork reaching
a height of 173 metres. It was defended from the north by a
steep hillside and a rampart, and on the other sides by two
ramparts. The entrance was on the east side and the gap to
the south overlooking Ludlow is recent. Storage pits have
been found all over the interior.

At one time it was thought that these **hillforts** were just
community retreats in emergencies. There is now evidence
that in spite of their exposed positions and lacking a source
of water within the enclosure, many were permanent settle-
ments. At Croft Ambrey near Leominster one camp was
occupied continuously between 550BC and 48 AD. Larger
ones were stoutly built defended towns with houses, stables,
granaries and temples. One thought provoking point has been
made; the average Iron Age hut had much the same floor area
as a modern two bedroom bungalow. Today Caynham Camp
is a secluded oval of sheep cropped grass within ramparts
still, on average, 10 feet high. It has a calm, beneficent
atmosphere and commands superb views.

The walk enters **Ludlow** beside the River Teme. This is a
lovely river but can be quite wild when the water is high,
see photo. The ordinary streets of ordinary houses on this
approach give no hint of what you can find in the town.
From Ludford Bridge stroll up Broad Street to explore
one of our oldest, liveliest, spiciest small towns.

The name Ludlow means 'the hill by the rapids', and
these two features, hill and river, account for its history.
Prehistoric and Roman roads crossed the river here, and
the defensible position of the hill made it a natural site for
a stronghold. The Teme flows on three sides and there is
a sharp ridge to the north and west. The Normans began
their castle late in the 12th century and planted a 'new
town' around it from which they could pacify and control
the turbulent Welsh. There are now buildings of all kinds
at some distance from the old centre, but until the 20th
century Ludlow barely reached beyond its mediaeval core.

Get a guidebook and the booklet describing the town's Discovery Trail. Certainly visit the castle and the big parish church of St Laurence, but most of all, just wander round the town centre. Most of the buildings are discreetly proportioned 18th century red brick or stucco, but there are many ornate timber framed buildings from the 15th century on, including some late Victorian Arts and Crafts.

Close your eyes if you pass the Tesco store, which blends with the rest of the town like a racing car in church. There are jettied upper floors, columns, oriels and gargoyles. The mixture of broad and narrow streets, cranks, alleys and strange corners is intricate, intimate and rewarding. This is a teeming town goggling with tourists.

You leave Ludlow across **Ludford Bridge,** a 15th century structure which replaced an earlier bridge. It has carried farmers, crops, animals, horses and carts and not least, trains of pack horses with Ludlow wool and cloth for Gloucester and Bristol. Until the bypass road was built the bridge took all the traffic travelling north or south.

The **best view** of Ludlow is from Whitcliffe Common across the Teme, a wooded cliff given to the town in the early 13th century. In the foreground stands the castle, the town lies behind it dominated by the tower of St Laurence's church against the distant backdrop of Titterstone Clee.

The Mortimer Trail comes highly recommended. From Dinham Bridge, the one downstream of Ludford Bridge, it travels 30 miles through the Marches through Oreleton Common, Aymestrey and Titley to Kington. If you have not heard of these places, perhaps that's the point of the walk. The route follows a series of south to west ridges but crosses the valleys of three rivers, the Teme, the Lugg and the Arrow. A county council booklet (ISBN 1 85301 021 9) gives full details. The cover shows a couple in shorts standing rather improbably up to their knees in bracken. He is pretending to consult a map but wears a lascivious grin.

(W117) Go R, cross bridge & take gate. Follow track 170 paces. Go half L off track heading 50 yds L of trees ahead, & cross mid-fence stile.

(W117a) Go R, follow hedge round field corner to next field corner, & cross stile.

(W118) Go half L to cross stile 25 yds above holly tree. Go ahead towards gap in earthwork to reach mid-hedge stile. DON'T CROSS.

[TO SEE Caynham Camp go ahead to earthwork.]

(W119) Go R to field corner gate & cross stile. Follow L hedge/fence round 2 top edges of field to opposite corner, & cross stile by gate onto track. ►

(E237a) Go R around 2 top edges of field to gate in opposite corner, & cross stile. Go ahead 50 yds to stile R. DON'T CROSS IT.

[TO SEE Caynham Camp cross stile to earthwork.]

(E238) Turn L heading 25 yds above holly tree, & cross stile. Bear L to small gate BUT CROSS STILE

(E239) Follow L hedge round field corner & cross stile L. Go half R down to track. Go R down track & take gate. ◄

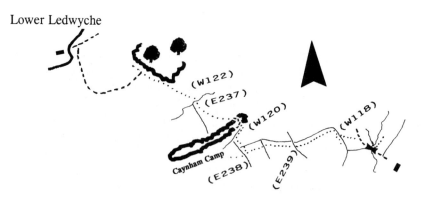

Lower Ledwyche

(W122)
(E237)
(W120)
(W118)
Caynham Camp
(E238)
(E239)

62

(W120) Go ahead down track (via gate) to open field.

(W121) Head for bottom L field corner, cross stream & take small gate.

(W122) Follow green track 200 yds & take track L. Go .5 mile (via R bend) & meet track. Go L to lane. ►

(E236) Go .5 mile (via L bend) to edge of wood. Go R down green track. [NB Rising field ahead has bulge of bushes in top hedge.] Cross stream.

(E237) Go up to R of bulgy bushes [brg 128] & join fenced track. Go 225yds (via gate & round R bend) to gate & cross stile. ◄

Ludford Bridge and the River Teme in flood

Ludlow Castle

63

(W123) Go ahead .3 mile to sharp L bend near pylon, & cross stile ahead.

(W124) Follow L hedge (via stile) then climb stile & bank to bypass. GREAT CARE

(W125) Cross to wooden post, descend bank & cross stile. Go L, round field corner & join fenced path to road. Go ahead up to T junction.

(W126) Cross road, go R 150 yds (past Blashfield Rd) & take tarmac footpath L. Follow (across 2 streets) to path junction with white railings.

(W127) Go L 250 yds (past stone path R) & take tarmac footpath R with concrete bollard.

(W128) Go 230 yds (across a road) to main road. GREAT CARE.

(W129) Cross, go R 100 yds & take Mary Elizabeth Rd. Go to bottom & join fenced path R. Cross railway & road to riverside road.

(W130) Go R .6 mile (at junctions go L) to Ludford Bridge.

Ludlow

(E229) Follow it across road and railway to bottom of a road. Go up to main road. DON'T CROSS HERE.

(E230) Go R 100 yds to No 10, cross road WITH CARE & take tarmac path opposite.

(E231) Go 230 yds (past playground & across road) to junction of paths with concrete bollard.

(E232) Go L 250 yds to path junction with white railings. Go R & cross 2 streets to main road.

(E233) Cross, go R 100 yds & take Coder Road L. Cross side road & take fenced path. Go round field corner plus 25 yds, & cross stile R.

(E234) Climb bank to bypass. GREAT CARE. Cross to wooden post, descend bank & cross stile. Follow R hedge (via stile) & cross stile to bend of road.

(E235) Go ahead .3 mile to L bend by house. Take track ahead 25 yds & take track R.

(E227) From town side of Ludford Bridge take river-side road. Go 180 yds & turn R on riverside road. Go 250 yds to tollhouse & turn R.

(E228) Go .3 mile to white railings L & take concrete path.

(E226) Go R on riverside path to green railings. Climb steps, follow path & go down steps to road. Go ahead to junction, then L to bridge.

Ludlow

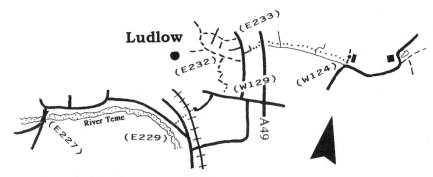

River Teme

Ludlow

(W131) From Ludford Bridge leave town on B4361 and take 1st road R. Climb steps & follow path to fork. Go R .4 mile to next bridge.

(W132) Take steps L to top & turn R. Follow path via more steps to top, then go ahead to road.

(W133) Go R to sharp bend. Take lane ahead for 25 yds & join rising path L. Follow it a few paces to fork, then go L 150 yds up to road.

(W134) Go L 50 yds & turn R onto track. Pass gate (North Farm), go on 30 yds & take earth track L.

(W135) Follow wood edge .6 mile & take tall gate.

(W136) Bear R & follow line of fence to cross-ways on corner of wood. Go R on sunken track 300 yds to hard track.

(W137) Cross & take sunken track (not parallel higher path) .3 mile, to project-ing corner of fence.

(W138) Go on with field on your L to T junction of paths. Go L (field on your L) to join track by gate.

(E218) Go L 2.4 miles to road.

(E219) Go L 350 yds & take wooden farm gate R.

(E220) Follow track 100 yds & fork L. Pass sheds on your L via gates. Climb track & take gate/stile. Go on to next gate, & take path on its L.

(E221) Follow it .5 mile (past 2 paths R, path L & path R) & join sunken track down to hard track.

(E222) Cross & take sunken track 300yds to crossways on corner of wood. Go L by fence to join track & take high wooden gate.

(E223) Follow wood edge path .6 mile to track.

(E224) Go R to road. Go L 50 yds to Mortimer Forest sign, & take small path R down to track. Go R to lane, then R to junction.

(E225) Fork R, go 100yds & take path L. Fork immed-iately L & follow path to take steps. Go on via more steps to river.

(W139) Go ahead (via 2 gate/stiles) to pass sheds on your R, then round R bend to gate & road.

(W140) Go L 350 yds & take track R (Hazel Coppice). Follow .9 mile to fork, & go L via gate. Go .9 mile & pass through farm.

(W141) Go on .5 mile & pass house (1) to house (2). Go 250 yds to start of concrete track. Go 50 yds & cross stile R. ◄

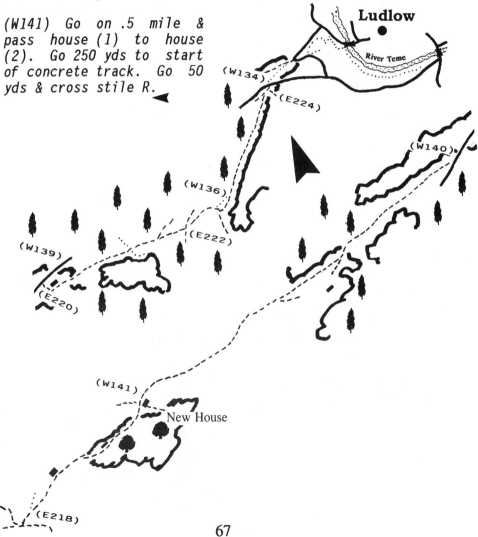

Ludlow

River Teme

(W134)

(E224)

(W140)

(W136)

(E222)

(W139)

(E220)

(W141)

New House

(E218)

From the long, straight track along the flank of **Bringewood Chase** there are magical views. Around you is blissful sheep country of small, green fields dotted with trees and valleys of golden gorse. In the distance are range upon range of blue and noble hills.

The **River Teme** rises in the Kerry Hills and runs 70 miles to join the Severn just south of Worcester. Before reaching Ludlow it has passed through only the small town of Knighton and the village of Leintwardine, so it a rural river with clean water.

Downstream of Leintwardine the Teme heads south-east for a few miles in a broad, looping reach known as the Leintwardine Fishery. At this point look at your Ordnance Survey map, because the river does an extraordinary thing. Instead of running south across the low lying land towards Amestry to join the Rivers Lugg and Wye, it turns north through the 300 metre high ridge of Bringewood Chase. It seems that before the last Ice Age the Teme did indeed flow south. However, at one period ice blocked its exit and the Teme formed a lake in the Vale of Wigmore. Eventually this overflowed to the north, cutting the spectacular Downton Gorge.

Castle Bridge in the Downton Gorge

Downton Castle

68

Downton Castle is first glimpsed as a distant promise standing grandly on the banks of the River Teme. You approach it through parkland laid out on the southern flank of the Gorge by Richard Payne Knight as a setting for his romantic extravaganza. Knight was an 18th century polymath, archaeologist, writer, bad poet and his own architect. The family had made money through the Shropshire iron trade and so Knight could indulge his fancies. However, he was an original thinker and did not accept currently fashionable notions of what a great house and its park should look like.

The late 18th century saw the start of a rebellion against the mannered and conventional classical forms that had dominated architecture since the begining of the century. This rational, carefully proportioned and symetrical architecture modelled on Greece and Rome was set in pastoral landscapes by Capability Brown and his like. Payne Knight condemned Brown's gentle rendering of nature. He sought the fierce and the terrible, craggy rocks, awsome caverns and jagged peaks. The houses fit to occupy these stern and brooding places would be mystical and romantic, and of course, these were the beginings of ideas that in the 19th century became the Romantic movement which inspired so many artists, poets, musicians and architects.

Downton Castle is one of our earliest Romantic buildings, preceded only by Vanburgh Castle and Strawberry Hill, the house of writer Horace Walpole which gave its name to early architecture of this type, Strawberry Hill Gothick. These early works were madly eclectic and not very scholarly, with random plunderings from English mediaeval buildings, Moorish architecture and anything else they fancied. Close to, it is obvious that the dramatic towers, turrets and oriel windows of Downton Castle are theatrical, not military. Somehow they look rather jokey, as though their builder was saying, 'I know that this is all terribly silly'. The tiny slits, or loops, look more useful for firing cupid's darts than arrows from a longbow. Nearby the Castle looks smaller and more apologetic than from the distant views.

(W142)Follow path to small gate & field. Go ahead parallel with L hedge to R side of big tree. Follow stream & cross footbridge.

(W143) Bear R, cross stile & climb to field corner. Go parallel with R hedge, pass midfield tree on your L & take gateway.

(W144) Bear L on earth track, curving R into field. Cross narrow part of field to bulge of bracken. Take path, cross stile & join track.

(W145) Go ahead up rising track to top, cross a track & take stile into field.

(W146) Go half R (head for middle of tree clump) & cross stile onto track. Go L 150 yds & cross stile L.

(W147) Go half R & down past midfield tree to cross stile. Take path through bracken onto stone track.

(W148) Go R .3 mile & take middle of 3 steel gates L.

(E212) Go L over bridge & follow track .4 mile (via bends & gates) to T junction of tracks.

(E213) Go R .35 mile to pass track L, plus 40 paces, & take small path L. Follow through bracken & cross stile to field.

(E214) Go half R to where mounds meet top fence, & cross stile onto track. Go R to gateway, plus 30 paces, & cross stile R.

(E215) Go half L heading (when in view) to midfence stile into wood. Go down to track junction & take falling track ahead.

(E216) Go to bottom & cross stile. Go ahead to edge of trees, then cross field at narrow point to meet earth track.

(E216) Follow round L bend & pass falling track R to take gateway. Go ahead to bottom L field corner. Take path to cross stile & then footbridge.

(E217) Go R to big tree. Go ahead to field edge power pole & take small gate. Go up wooded path & cross stile onto track.

(W149) Follow track down & round bends to cross bridge. Go ahead & take gate/stile R.

(W150) Go .4 mile (past castle) to draw level with timber framed house R.

(W151) Go R & down to cross stile. Go L to track. Go R 25yds to just past house & take gate L.

(W152) Follow green path, bearing L to join banked path. Follow (via gate) .3 mile to bridge & lane. ▶

(E209) Go .3 mile (via gate) till track vanishes, then bear L past big oak & take gate onto track.

(E210) Go R 25 yds past house, take track L a few yds & cross stile R. Go ahead to join track.

(E211) Go L .4 mile (past castle) & take gate/stile. ◀

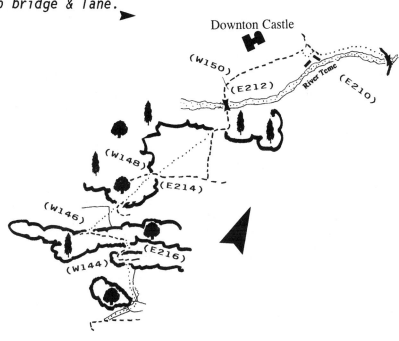

(W153) Go L 150 yds & take track L. Go 75 yds to pass houses & take path R up to field.

(W154) Go half L to L end of long tree clump, & take stile to lane. (IF BLOCK-ED map shows way round.)

(W155) Go L .5 mile to red phone box, plus 100 yds, & go R up farm drive.

(W156) Go between build-ings & take 2 gates into field. Go ahead to corner of barn, then half L past big oak to projecting fence corner.

(W157) Keep fence on your L & follow green track .5 mile to take gate.

(W158) Follow green track 150 yds to meet stone track. Go half L up field to lone stile by top fence

(W159) Follow L fence (via L kink) .5 mile (via gate/ stile), & take gate onto track.

(W160) Follow to junction by house. Go L (via gate) to lane. Go R to main road

(W161) Don't cross. Go L 100yds, take track L for 5 paces & take woodland track R.▶

(E201) Go R 100 yds to crossroads. Go R 25 yds & take track L.

(E202) Go 100 yds & take track R 300 yds to field corner. Take L of 2 gates.

(E203) Follow R hedge/ fence .5 mile (via gate/ stile), bearing L to pass projecting fence corner & on to lonely stile.

(E204) Go half L down to midfield tree, cross rising stone track & follow level earth track to take gate.

(E205) Follow track .5 mile (parallel with R fence) to fence corner by big oak near farm. Go to L end of long barn & take gate. Take drive to road.

(E206) Go L .5 mile to The Brakes, plus 150 yds to cross stile R.

(E207) IF FIELD obstructed map shows lane alternative

Go half L to biggest tree, heading (when in view) for R side of house, to reach field corner. Take path to track.

(E208) Go L to lane. Go R down to nearside of bridge & take green track R. ◀

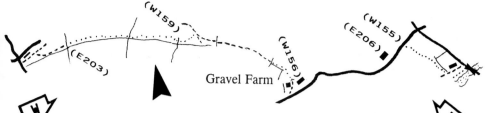

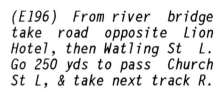

Gravel Farm

(W162) Follow down to wood edge & take gate into field.

(W163) Go ahead, bearing L to follow L fence to field end. Go ahead through gappy hedge. Go on with hedge on your R to field corner, & take gate onto track.

(W164) Go ahead to gate & lane. Go L .25 mile through farm to house R, & take kissing gate R.

(W165) Follow wall then L hedge to field corner, & take kissing gate. Go ahead midfield & take gate -way. Follow R hedge to corner, take gate/stile & join track to street.

(W166) Go L down to T junction & R to bridge at

Leintwardine

Leintwardine

(E196) From river bridge take road opposite Lion Hotel, then Watling St L. Go 250 yds to pass Church St L, & take next track R.

(E197) Go to end & cross stile AHEAD. Follow L hedge, bearing R to take gateway. Go ahead & take small gate. Follow R hedge to small gate & lane.

(E198) Go L .25 mile & take gate R onto hedged track.

(E199) Go 300 yds to sharp R bend & take gate ahead. Follow L hedge to field corner & go ahead through gappy hedge.

(E200) Go ahead & follow R hedge to field end, bearing L to take gate. Follow woodland track .4 mile (at fork go L) up to track. Go L to road.

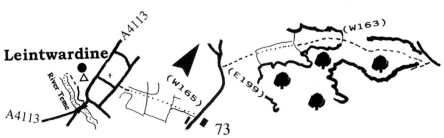

Leintwardine dozes on a slope above the confluence of the River Clun with the River Teme. There was once a small Roman settlement here, Bravinium, but it's been pretty quiet since then. The buildings are mainly in a soft looking local limestone which must surely be porous. The biggest structure is the huge tower of the Church of St Mary Magdalene, a fine lofty church with a hammer-beam roof sprouting intricately carved bosses. There are beautiful 15th century oak choir stalls. The intense, rich colours of the east window of 1860 contrast with the strong, simple work in the modern window by the pulpit. Both are much more to my taste than the pale and pious figures in the south wall of 1892 and the fantasy knights in armour next to them from 1915. The foundations, as with many churches, are Saxon and Norman, but most of what you see is 13th or 14th century.

Flatlands are those reedy, watery places where skeins of little brooks converge and trickle through beds of cressy, green weed. They are hardly tough walking country but they have an appeal of their own. The only one I can offer you on this book is just west of Leintwardine and it lasts for only a couple of miles. The Teme is in a hurry, a busy, brisk river, but this area drains into the Clun which loops and lingers between its banks of alders and willows.

Bedstone is a tiny settlement but it was recorded in the Domesday Book, though under a different name because at that time they had not invented spelling. The village has the air of a company town. Not only do the staff and students of Bedstone College quite outnumber the natives, but the village seems never to have been more than an accessory to the great house. The vastly proportioned, half timber and Welsh brick, black and white striped, betturreted, multi chimnied high Victorian dream palace which is the College was formerly Bedstone Court (1884).

Near the College entrance is an attractive range of three timber dutch barns. Pocket sized St Mary's church is the sucessor to a chapel built before the Norman conquest and the present building is of Norman origin. It has a Saxon font. The church wears a square, timber framed bellcote with a magnificent weathervane like an enormous hat.

The **forest** west of Bedstone seems to be planted mainly with conifers, but the walk initially follows a track along the edge which has quite a rich flora. You can probably improve on my hasty and inexpert list of birch, black-thorn, oak, ash, sycamore, elder, small leaved lime, wild rose, gorse, hawthorn, wild cherry, honeysuckle, hazel, bracken, nettles, foxgloves, brambles and thistles.

There is nothing of **Stowe** but a very small church, but it was once a meeting point on drovers' roads from Wales to England. The church of St Michael & All Angels is a mediaeval construction with a fine timber roof. The churchyard is oval, which is usually thought to suggest a pagan site taken over by the church.

Approaching Knighton you walk through **Kinsley Wood**. Most of it seems to be conifers, but this lower edge has beech, sycamore, a few Scots pine, larch, cypress, and a good many of the American red oak. This tree grows faster than our native oaks and produces good timber, though not as durable as ours. In autumn it is the glory of the woodlands as its flaming yellow, red and orange leaves slowly fall.

75

Leintwardine

(W167) Take Mill Lane between garage & post office for .25 mile (after gate it becomes track) & cross bridge L.

(W168) Go R by river through fields (1) and (2). In (3) keep ahead on same line (as river bears R) to L end of field-end fence, & cross small footbridge (NOT gated culvert)

(W169) Go L by hedge 200 yds & cross footbridge L. Cross stile into field. Follow L fence to field corner & take gate.

(W170) Go ahead to L of poplars & take gate onto track. Go R across bridge plus 100 yds (via gate), & take gate L.

▶

(E192) Go R via gate & bridge to poplars, & take gate L. Bear L to L side of bush & take gate.

(E193) Follow R fence to field end, bearing L to cross stile. Cross footbridge, go R to field corner & cross footbridge.

(E194) Go half L, curving R to walk parallel with L field edge, & take kissing gate. Keep ahead .4 mile (via kissing gate) & cross bridge L onto track.

(E195) Go R .25 mile into

Leintwardine

◀

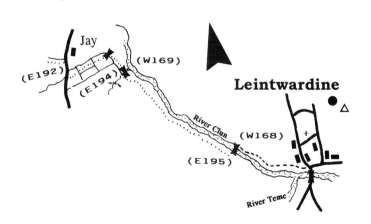

(W171) Follow R hedge past gate R & take field-end gate. Pass gate L, follow L FENCE past houses to field corner, & cross wooden fence.

(W172) Follow L hedge to field corner & cross wooden fence onto track. *(Fence might be concealed by vegetation.)*

(W173) Go R .75 miles to road.

(W174) Go R 250 yds & take lane L to College gate. Go R *(not sharp R)* on rising lane, & pass church to T junction. ►

(E188) Go R a few paces, take lane past church & curve R to junction. Go L *(not sharp L)* to B4367.

(E189) Go R 250 yds & take track L. Follow .75 mile to 6 paces from its end.

(E190) Cross wooden fence L into field. *(Corner may be overgrown.)* Follow R hedge to field corner & cross wooden fence.

(E191) Follow R fence past houses to field corner & take middle of 3 gates. Follow L hedge past gate L to field corner, & take gate onto track. ◄

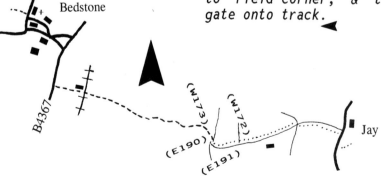

Adleymoor Common

77

(W175) Go R 10 paces & take hedged track up to gate & field. Follow R hedge to field corner & take gate into open field.

(W176) Bear R to far R field corner & take gate. Cross summit & (when in view) head for end of tree line R, & take gate.

(W177) Follow green track up to hard track. Go L .3 mile to fork. Go L via gates, pass house, & exit onto track.

(W178) Go R & take gate into forest. Follow hard track to sharp R bend. Keep ahead up green track for .3 mile to track junction at crest. ▶

(E184) Go L 12 paces & take falling green track R .3 mile to track bend. Go R, take forest edge gate & go down to house.

(E185) Enter gateway, go R (via 2 gates) up to track. Go R .3 mile to stone track L, & turn R down green track.

(E186) Go to its end & take gate. Bear L to put row of trees on your L, then go parallel with them to field end & take gate.

(E187) Bear R to 2 gates and take R one. Follow L hedge to gate & track. Go down to lane at Bedstone. ◀

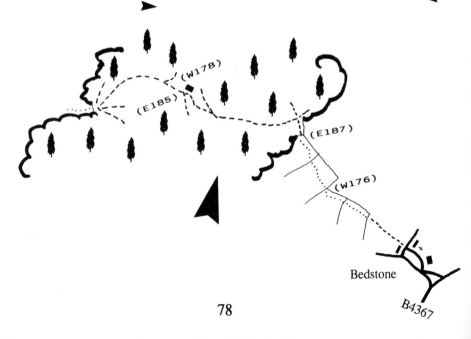

Bedstone

B4367

(W179) Bear L to steel gate & take kissing gate. Follow L fence/hedge .5 mile (via gates/stiles & past farm) to take gate above white house. Pass house on your R & join drive down to road.

(W180) Go R 75 yds & take lane L. Go through farm via 2 gates, then curve L & take gate.

(W181) Follow rising stone track 1 mile (via gates & farm), to pass line of conifers R & meet track. Take gate R.

(W182) Follow track .5 mile to corner of forest where track turns R. Keep ahead by R fence & take gate. ►

(E180) Follow L fence & join track for .5 mile to take gate.

(E181) Go L by L fence & join track for 1 mile. Pass 1st farm L & go on to curve R through 2nd farm to road.

(E182) Go R 75 yds & take drive L. At fork go R up to white house, leaving drive to pass it on your L & take gate.

(E183) Follow green track .5 mile via gate/stiles & past farm. When it peters out follow R fence to kissing gate & junction of hard tracks. ◄

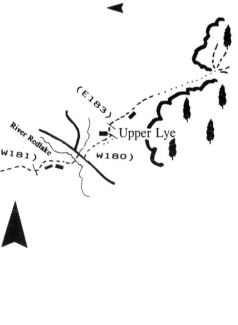

79

(W183) Go half L [brg 290]
(past fence corner & pond
on your L & drawing away
from forest L) to meet
track.

(W184) Follow track down
small valley .25 mile (via
gate) to pond.

(W185) Pass pond & curve
down L .4 mile (via gate)
to crosstracks.

(W186) Go down R past
church to junction. Go R
past Old Vicarage gate &
take gated track to a few
paces from cattle grid.

(W187) Take gate L & go up
rising green hollow by R
fence to meet track.

(W188) Take gate opposite
& follow L hedge via 2
gates to 3rd. Follow R
hedge to gate & lane.

(W189) Go L a few paces &
cross stile. Cross foot-
bridge, then head for far
bottom field corner &
cross stile. Take steps
up to hard track.

➤

(E175) Go parallel with R
fence towards end of
trees, then bear L to
cross footbridge, & stile
onto lane.

(E176) Go L 8 paces & take
gate. Follow L hedge &
take gate. Follow R hedge
(via 2 gates) & take top
gate onto track.

(E177) Cross & go down
green hollow by L fence
(via gate) to track. Go R
& take gate onto lane.
Take lane L past church to
track junction.

(E178) Curve L & follow
main track up .4 mile
(via gate) to pass pond L.
Curve up L (via gate) .25
mile to field, where track
peters out.

(E179) As track ends, turn
half L [brg 30]. Pass pond
& fence corner on your R
to reach field corner, &
take gate.

◄

Town Clock

St Michael & All Angels, Stowe

(W184)

(E179)

(W185)

Stowe

(W187)   (E178)

(E177)

(W190)

A488

(E175)

E

Knighton

Knighton

● △

A488

(W190) Go R 100 yds to R
bend & take green track L.
Follow .4 mile to road.

(W191) Go ahead 150 yds &
take road R. Cross railway
and go to town centre ►

Knighton

(E173) From town clock go
downhill 100 yds & take
road L to station. Go .25
mile & cross railway to
junction. Go R 150 yds &
take rising track L.

(E174) Follow it .4 mile
to bend of track. Go R
100 yds to R bend & take
steps down to stile &
field. ◄

Knighton is a small and agreeable market town on a hill which is dominated by a big clock. There are several of these around mid Wales and this one is a delicious gothic fantasy. The other prominent structure is the church of King Edward the Confessor. There was certainly a church on the site in the 11th century and probably much earlier. The oldest part of the building is Norman but most of it is Victorian. The squat and secretive bellcote houses a peal of eight bells. Knighton stands on a crossing of the River Teme and forms a gateway between the level, prosperous country around Ludlow and the hilly Welsh borderlands. It is not surprising that there has been a settlement here since the Stone Age.

Offa's Dyke was build by the king of Mercia in the 700s to defend his border in the interminable warfare with the Welsh. The true extent and alignment of this great rampart are unclear. It seems never to have extended further north than Wrexham, and in the south it is only visible today in short sections. The Dyke may been built after negotiation with the Welsh princes in a period of relative calm. That Offa could organise and finance such a project is an amazing demonstration of his power and wealth.

Knighton is midway on the famous Offa's Dyke Path (173 miles) between Prestatyn on the North Wales coast and Chepstow on the Bristol Channel. Visit the Offa's Dyke Centre in the town for information.

According to a local information leaflet, the second main event in Knighton's history was the building of the scenically splendid **Heart of Wales Line**. The railway runs 110 miles between Shrewsbury and Llanelli and was built in fragments between 1828 and 1868. It allowed Knighton to become a distribution centre for fertilizer, cattle feed and seed, and it stimulated cloth making, tanning and malting. The line also allowed the London & North Western Railway to carry coal from South Wales into central and northern England. During World War I it had the vital role of supplying coal to the Navy at Scapa Flow.

From Knighton you follow the same route as **Llwybr Owain Glyndwr** to Llangunllo, though until a recent rerouting the LOG ran north-west from Bailey Hill. This magnificent walk through hill and moorland scenery visits places associated with Glyndwr's 15th century rebellion against English rule.

In the early 1980s I noted that **St Michael's Pool** had almost silted up and vanished, but it is not much different today and still about to vanish. Do the banks look as though they were built up at some time to hold more water? If so, for what purpose?

The English translation of **Cwm y Gaist** is obscure. Cwm is a shallow valley and for the rest, 'treasure' has been suggested. The small chapel was built in 1863 by the Primitive Methodists but was converted to a private house almost 30 years ago when the congregation had dwindled to two. The striking white finish is not an innovation, it was always white, I was once invited inside and found the main living room to be a single large space with a wooden gallery at first floor level.

Chapel, Cwm y Gaist

LNWR 2-4-2 tank engine and typical LNWR coaches from a postcard pre 1923

Knighton

(W192) From town clock go downhill & take lane R between George & Dragon and HSBC.

(W193) Go .3 mile (past lane R, lane becomes path) to junction with lane.

(W194) Go ahead 20 paces & take rising path R. Cross stile, pass end of road & follow hedged path to road

(W195) Cross, go L up ramp to wall & take path R. Go up & cross stile onto bend of lane.

(W196) Go ahead 25 paces & cross stile L. Follow L hedge (via stile) to hedge corner. Go ahead on green track down to sheds on L bend.

(W197) Leave track, go ahead between trees & keep this line to meet projecting hedge corner.

(W198) Go with hedge on your L .5 mile (over stile & past cow shed R), till fence drops L. Go ahead down to stile & lane.

▶

(E168) Follow track (becomes lane) for 1 mile. Pass white farm plus 50yds & take L spur to next lane

(E169) Go R 50 yds & cross stile. Follow rising path to join R fence, then go .5 mile (past cowshed L & over stile) till fence bends R. Keep ahead to sheds & join track.

(E170) Go up ahead (past L fork) till track bends L. Keep ahead past projecting hedge corner & cross stile. Follow R hedge & cross stile onto lane.

(E171) Go R 25 paces to L bend, cross stile & follow path down to road. Go L 25 paces & take path R.

(E172) Pass end of road, cross stile & go down to lane. Go ahead 20 paces & take lane R. Follow it .3 mile (past L fork) to

Knighton

◀

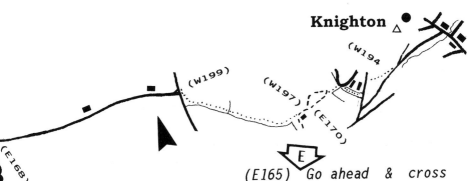

Knighton

(W194)

(W199)

(W197)

(E170)

(E168)

E

(E165) Go ahead & cross cattle grid. Take track opposite & cross next grid. Bear R into field, then turn L. Follow L fence (via gate) to field corner, & take gate.

W

(W199) Go R 50 yds & take spur L to lane. Go R past farm 1 mile (lane becomes track) to gate across track.

(W200) Follow R hedge to stream & take gate. Follow track 300 yds to track junction.

(W201) Go L on track & follow L fence/hedge 1.25 miles (via gates, past pond L & end of conifers R) to gate onto hard track R. DON'T TAKE IT.

(W202) Go ahead on green track & take gate. Follow R fence (via gate) down to field corner, then join hard track R.

(E166) Go ahead past cattle grid & join fenced green track. Follow track & R fence 1.25 miles (via gates) to fourway track junction with finger post.

(E167) Go R, take gate & cross stream. Follow L hedge & take gate by conifers.

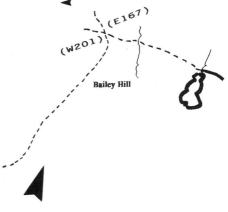

(E167)

(W201)

Bailey Hill

(E166)
(W202)

Cefn-suran

85

W

(W203) Go ahead to track junction. Cross cattle grid & follow drive 60 yds to L bend.

(W204) Go ahead, take path through trees & cross stile onto track. Go L through gateway plus 25 paces, then turn R on rising track.

(W205) Take gate, rise to conifer clump & take gate. Go ahead (leaving R hedge) to bottom of conifers, & take gate. Follow fenced path to field. Go ahead & cross stile.

(W206) Go half R & take gate onto lane. Go L 100 yds & cross stile R. Go ahead to markpost, then down sunken path to open field.

(W207) Go ahead to cross track & stile. Bear R & follow R hedge (via gate), & take gate onto path. Go to road then R into

Llangunllo

[IF just passing through, route continues via gate behind road sign at para (W209)]

Llangunllo

(E159) From War Memorial take road past post box. Go 450yds (crossing river) & take drive L.

(E160) Go 20 paces & take hedged path up to gate & field. Follow L hedge & take gate. Go ahead, bearing R to cross stile in top fence, onto track.

(E161) Go ahead, bearing R beside trees & join sunken path. Follow it to top R field corner & cross stile onto lane.

(E162) Go L 100 yds & take gate R. Bear L to 1st tree & cross stile. Go ahead to bottom of conifers, join fenced track & take gate.

(E163) Go ahead to R side of conifer clump, & take gate. Follow track towards farm & take gate.

(E164) Go to end of L fence & turn L. Go ahead through gateway plus 15 paces, & cross stile R. Go through trees & join farm drive. ◄

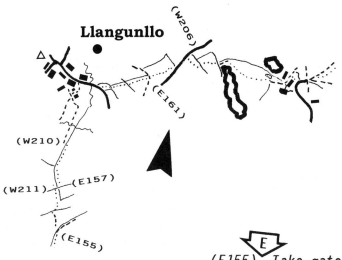

Llangunllo

(W206)

(E161)

(W210)

(W211) (E157)

(E155)

W

(W208) From War Memorial take road past post box for 150 yds. Take rising track by road sign & go through gate.

(209W) Follow track R between barns, then turn L. Take falling track L, curve R & go up 200 yds to cross ditch.

(W210) Go on 70 paces & take gate L/below. Go R by fence to crest & take gate R, then gate L.

(W211) Follow L fence till it bends L, then keep ahead down to take gate. Go ahead up line of sunken track, then bear R & take gate onto end of earth track. ▶

E

(E155) Take gate ahead & follow sunken track into field. Pass midfield tree, follow old track down & take gate.

(E156) Go half R on green track past projecting fence corner & follow R fence to field corner.

(E157) Take gate & turn R through 2nd gate. Go L down fence to bottom field corner & take gate L. Go R down earth track, curving L to pass barns & take gate.

(E158) Go R (via 2 gates) & follow track L to gate & road.

[IF just passing though the route continues R.]

◀ **Llangunllo**

87

(W212) Go ahead at 90 deg from gate [or brg 204] & (when in view) head for R field corner & take gate by water trough. Follow R fence to field corner & take gate R.

(W213) Follow fenced strip & take gate. Follow R fence (via gate) to conifers R, & take gate.

(W214) Follow track .4 mile down to crosstracks.

(W215) Go L .6 mile (past conifer clump with shed) to T junction of tracks.

(W216) Take gate R & follow track .5 mile (down steep curve) to track junction by stream.

(W217) Go R & up .25 mile to meet lane.

(W218) PATH AHEAD MAY BE OBSTRUCTED by a bog and a barbed wire fence. If so, you are allowed to take a resonable detour. ►

(E149) Take rough falling track .25 mile (via gate) & cross stream to T junction.

(E150) Go L & up (via gate) to pass pool L & take either of 2 gates.

(E151) Go L .6 mile (past conifer clump & shed) to crossroads.

(E152) Take track R .4 mile (past end of conifers R) & take gate by conifers L.

(E153) Follow L fence (via gate) & take gate into fenced strip. Go to far end & take gate.

(E154) Go L down fence to field corner & take gate by water trough. Go half R & (when in view) head for nearest end of earth track. DON'T FOLLOW IT. ◄

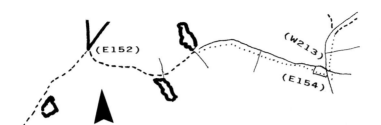

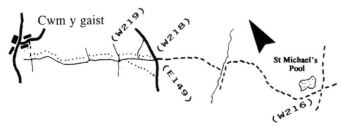

IF CLEAR: Take gate opposite, follow L fence through conifers to field corner, & take gate ahead.

IF BLOCKED: Take gate L, go 75yds & take gate R. Go half R & take midfence gate. Go L to field corner & take gate.

(W219) Follow L fence (via gates) till fence ends. Go ahead with sunken track on your L, curving R then L, & take gate ahead. Go on by track 100 yds, then curve R down holloway to village.

(E146) Follow sunken track 100yds to projecting fence corner R. Turn L & walk beside sunken track (via gate, then R & L bends) to take gate.

(E147) Follow R fence via gates (1) & (2) UP TO midfence gate R.

(E148) PATH AHEAD MAY BE OBSTRUCTED by a bog and a barbed wire fence. If so you are allowed to make a reasonable detour.

IF CLEAR go ahead through conifers & take gate onto lane.

IF BLOCKED take gate R, go half L & take midfence gate onto track. Go L & take gate to junction.

(W220) Go L to T junction.
Go L 75 yds & take track R
(becomes grass track).
Cross railway & take gate
into field.

(W221) Bear L to middle of
bottom fence, cross stream
& take R of 2 gates.

(W222) Follow L fence (via
gate) & take gate onto
green track. Go ahead,
bearing L past midfield
tree. When in view, head
for bungalow & meet track.

(W223) Go R & cross cattle
grid. [NB Bracken on the
common can be a problem in
summer. Choose your option
depending on bracken, on
visibility and your skill
with a compass.]

EITHER go half L past
projecting hedge corner
[brg 250] & cross common
to join unfenced road. Go
R to cattle grid.

OR follow track to meet
road. Go R .5 mile to
cattle grid.

[NB The route runs across
the common but bracken
can be a problem in
summer. Choose your option
depending on bracken,
visibility and your skill
with a compass.]

(E141) EITHER take brg 68
& cross common to cattle
grid on track,

OR Follow road .5 mile &
take track R. Follow to
cattle grid.

(E142) Follow track 100
yds to house. Go half L
past midfield tree & take
gate in bottom fence.

(E143) Follow R hedge (via
gate) to field bottom,
take gate & cross stream.

(E144) Go half L up
curving hollow & take
gate. Cross railway &
follow track to lane.

(E145) Go L 75 yds & turn
R. Go 50 yds to pass tim-
ber shed R & take gate R.

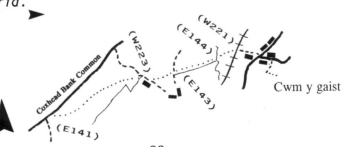

Cwm y gaist

90

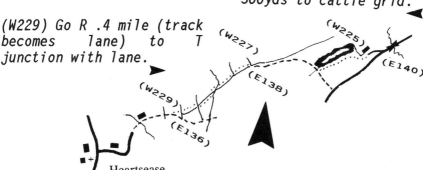

W ◄

(W224) Go ahead 300 yds to cross river & take 2nd gate R (Dolyfelin). Follow drive to house & opposite glazed porch, take 2nd small gate L.

(W225) Go half R & cross stream, then bear R to join R fence. Follow it to top of conifers & meet track.

(W226) Go R through gate & follow track .25 mile (via gate (1)) & bend R through gate (2).

(W227) Go L by L fence to field corner & cross fence. Go on pass 1st gate L & cross stream, plus 200 yds, to take 2nd gate L.

(W228) Go R along hedge to field corner & take gate R. Go L along hedge to field corner & through gappy hedge to next field. Go half L & take gate onto track.

(W229) Go R .4 mile (track becomes lane) to T junction with lane.

E ▼

(E135) Take lane opposite, round L bend (becomes byway), go down past white cottage & take 1st gate. Go on 300 yds & take 2nd gate.

(E136) Go 25 paces & take, gate L. Go half R & through gappy hedge into next field. Follow R hedge to field corner & take gate R.

(E137) Go L along fence & take gate L. Go R by fence, cross a fence & take next gate R.

(E138) Follow track 400yds to top of conifers L, & take gate.

(E139) Go down L by trees & (when in view) head for R side of house. Cross stream & take small gate onto drive.

(E140) Go to road. Go L 300yds to cattle grid.

Heartsease

91

(W230) Go L a few paces &
enter farm. Go L between
sheds, turn sharp R &
follow track via gates to
field.

(W231) Follow R hedge via
2 gates, then follow L
hedge & join track to far
end of steel sheds.

(W232) Go R a few paces to
lane & turn L. Pass
buildings on your L & take
gate. Follow track down
to next gate.

(W233) Go ahead 50yds &
turn L. Follow track .4
mile to its end by stream.

(W234)Go ahead with trees/
hedge on your R to gate &
hedged track. Go ahead
through conifers, plus .25
mile, to track T junction.

(W235) Go R & follow track
to road. Go L 300yds to
church.

Llanddewi
Ystradenni ►

Llanddewi
Ystradenni

(E129) Face church gates &
go R 300 yds (past farm)
to house with red iron
leanto, & take track R

(E130) Go .3 mile (via
sharp L bend & R bend) &
take track L.

(E131) Go .4 mile (via
conifers) to end of hedged
section, & take gate.

(E132) Follow L hedge to
field corner, take gate &
cross stream. Follow track
.4 mile to track T
junction.

(E133) Go R via 2 gates to
farm. Pass buildings on
your R, take track R & go
through gate.

(E134) Turn L up side of
steel sheds, follow track
till it ends & take gate.
Follow L hedge (via gates)
into farm, & go through
yard to lane.

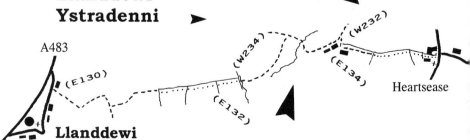

A483

(E130)

Llanddewi
Ystradenni

(W232)

(W234)

(E134)

Heartsease

(E132)

92

Llanddewi Ystradenni

(W236) Face church gates & go L to A483. Go L 300yds, cross river & take lane R. Go 300yds, pass house gate L & take track L.

(W237) Go .5 mile & pass 1st & 2nd tracks L to sharp R bend near houses.

****

TEMPORARY ROUTE

The Right of Way was blocked in two places on my last visit. The law allows you to take a reasonable detour, as follows. Phone 01926 776363 to see if the path has been cleared.

(W238T) Leave track & go ahead by L hedge to rejoin track. Go through gateway to sharp L bend. Leave track, follow R hedge to field corner & take gate R

(W239T) Go half L & take midhedge gate onto lane. Go R 150 yds to gates & (bust?) stiles each side, & take L gate/stile.

MAIN ROUTE RESUMES ►
****

****

TEMPORARY ROUTE

Right of Way was blocked in two places on my last visit. The law allows you to make a reasonable detour, as follows. Phone 01926 776363 to check present position.

(E125T) Go R 150 yds & take gate L opposite power pole. Go half R to bottom field corner & take R of 2 gates.

(E126T) Go L up hedge & join track. Go ahead through gateway, then leave track & follow R hedge to rejoin track. Go ahead.

MAIN ROUTE RESUMES
****

(E127) Go .5 mile to lane.

(E128) Go R 300 yds to A483. Go L 300 yds (past track R), & take road R to church gates.

◄ Llanddewi Ystradenni

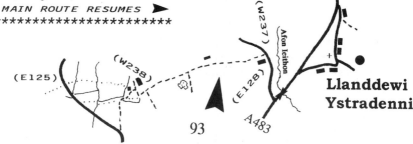

93

Cwm Aran is the beautiful, steep, wooded valley of the Afon Aran which lies a few hundred yards to the west of Coxhead Bank Common. Where the river crosses the southern end of the Common is the site of a castle with a Norman style Motte and Bailey. All that remains are steep ramparts and in the centre, a small farm. Some 700 yards west on a hilltop and just to the south of this walk is a 'camp', again with fortifications, but smaller. We can only wonder about their purpose so long ago in this desolate, infertile place.

Llanddewi Ystradenni is now correctly spelt on recent maps, but is still wrong on some road signs. For centuries Welsh names have been anglicised, but now we are seeing the country and its language treated with more respect. I have used the Welsh spellings where the anglicised name is just a corruption of the original. Where places have a genuine English name I have used whichever is better known. So Knighton is a more familiar label for that little border town than Tref y Clawdd. Rhaeadr, on the other hand, has simply been mangled.

Llanddewi may now be spelt correctly, but is still seems rather lost. Its only pub has shut and there are no shops, Post Office or school. The little church was rebuilt in 1890 seems rather sad too, under its wooden bellcote. The outside is not distinguished, but inside it is light with windows of tinted rather than stained glass. Brass paraffin lamps hang from brackets over the pews and the whole effect is calm and pleasing.

There are two fine **view points** on the way to Rhaeadr. The hill south of the forests around Abbeycwmhir seems to have no particular name, but 'Black Bank' appears on the southern flank. There are rewarding views of the miles of hills to the south, particularly the Radnor Forest. This huge plateau is some 660 metres high in the centre and marked off from the surrounding land by steep slopes. Streams drain off it in all directions and the deep valleys cut its circular mass into segments, like a rotting tree stump.

Gwastedyn Hill is the second viewpoint. Overlooking Rhaeadr from the south-east, its summit reaches 477 metres. As you climb towards the bare top the summit of Gwastedyn lies ahead. To the west the mountain road to Aberystwyth snakes up between high bluffs onto the moors. To the south-west is Cwm Elan, a long valley reaching towards the reservoirs. To the north-west and north-east are range upon range of hills with misty hints of further giants beyond. To the east is Hay Bluff, the top of the Radnor Forest, the Black Mountains and the Brecon Beacons.

From Rhaeadr this walk follows the **Wye Valley Walk** for a few miles. The confluence of the rivers Elan and Gwy is very attractive, with a crazy footbridge (pictured) over the Elan. There are several ways of crossing from Rhaeadr to the Claerwen Dam, the departure point for crossing the great, wet, green desert known as the Elynedd. I chose this route as the most rewarding because it avoids low level circuits around the reservoirs, which become remarkably tedious.

Footbridge over Afon Elan

Triangle Inn, Rhaeadr

95

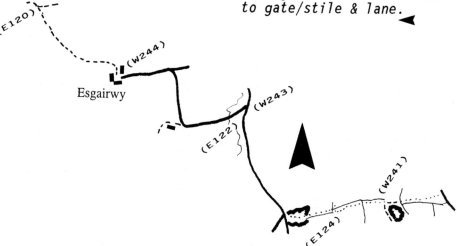

(W240) Follow L fence/ hedge to FIELD CORNER & take gate onto track. Go to end of hedged section where track bends L.

(W241) Go ahead by R fence to field corner & take gate ahead. Go ahead with bank/ditch on your L, pass through small wood & take gate onto lane.

(W242) Go R .5 mile (past phone box) & take lane L.

(W243) Go .7 mile (cross river, at 1st junction go R, at 2nd go L) & enter farmyard.

(W244) Go R between sheds & take track curving L. Go .4 mile & take gate onto T junction of tracks.

(E120) Go .4 mile to farm & turn R through yard to join lane.

(E121) Follow tarmac .7 mile (at 1st junction go R, at 2nd go L) to road.

(E122) Go R .5 mile to falling lane R, & take black steel gate into wood opposite (L).

(E123) Go ahead .4 mile with sunken track/ditch on your R to cross ditch from L, & take gate R.

(E124) Go L by hedge, join hedged track to its end & take gate. Follow R fence to gate/stile & lane.

Esgairwy

(W245) Go L 150 yds to corner of forest R. Bear R off track & follow path with forest on your R, to gate. Cross stile onto forest track.

(W246) Go 300 yds till track ends at markpost. Turn 90deg L & take path down to cross stream.

(W247) Go ahead across grass, but bear R & follow edge of trees for 250 yds, then rise onto stone track.

(W248) Go ahead, pass buildings on your L & follow curving track .5 mile to junction.

(W249) Go L 300yds curving L & then R onto shoulder of hill, & take steep rough track R.

(W250) Go up 400 yds onto stone track.

(W251) Turn R, take L fork 400 yds to markpost, & take rough track L.

(W252) Go to fence, then R beside it to gate, & cross stile. ►

(E114) Go R up fence to gate & cross stile onto rough track. Go R & round L bend to stone track.

(E115) Go R 400 yds to junction with markpost. Leave stone tracks & take STEEP ROUGH track 400 yds down to stone track.

(E116) Go L 300 yds down to track junction, then R .5 mile to buildings.

(E117) Pass them on your R plus 50 paces, to R bend. Leave track, follow edge of trees for 250 yds into corner of forest, then bear L & cross stream.

(E118) Go ahead on small path to green track with markpost. Go R 300 yds (past fork L) to forest edge, & cross stile.

(E119) Go ahead with trees on your L to earth track. Go L 150 yds to track junction & take gate R. ◄

(W253) Follow L fence & take 1st gate L. Go on down fence but bear L to thorn bush (round rough ground), then go down R to cross stream & take gate.

(W254) Follow rough track up bank & go L to pass trees on your L. Track becomes clear again, follow it 1.2 miles (becomes stone track) up to gate onto lane by conifer clump. DON'T TAKE GATE.

(W255) Turn R & go parallel with conifers 75 yds, to meet trough & line of trees leading R.

(W256) Follow them .35 mile over shoulder of hill & go down to join track.

(W257) Follow it through 2 gates & farm, plus 150 yds, & take gated track L. Go down & take next gate.

(W258) Go ahead a few paces to avoid mud, then go R parallel with hedge & stream to field corner. Go ahead through gate (if present, otherwise cross fence) & join track. ►

(E106) Follow L hedge & cross stream. Go ahead up field & take gate onto track.

(E107) Go L a few paces then take track R down to cross stream. Bear L off track (following stream) & cross fence (or take gate if present) into field corner.

(E108) Go parallel with stream to field corner & take gate L onto track. Go up to meet a track.

(E109) Go R through farm & take 2 gates. Go on 300 yds & take rising track L.

(E110) Follow it (as trough in ground) .35 mile over shoulder of hill, to conifers. Go L to track.

(E111) Go up L .65 mile (ignore gated fork L) to end of stone track, & take gate into field.

(E112) Follow R fence .3 mile to its end. Go ahead on grass track past conifers & take gate R.

(E113) Cross stream, go R around thorn bush (avoids rough ground), then bear L to join fence & take gate. ◄

(W)

(W259) Go R & up to meet track. Go L a few paces & take gate R. Go ahead & (when in view) head for where hedge & stream meet. Cross stream & follow hedge to gate & lane.

(W260) Go R .4 mile (past house R) & take track L.

(W261) Go .5 mile via 1st gate & take 2nd gate. Go on 200 yds, round sharp R bend, plus 25 yds, & take gate L.

(W262) Ignore track, follow L hedge (via bust (?) gate) to cattle grid, & join stone track.

(W263) Go L .5 mile (track becomes lane) to cross-roads.

Black Bank

(W254) (E113)

(W256) (E111)

Yr Onnen

(E105)

(W258)

(E108)

(W260)

(W262) Great Castle

(E104)

A44

(E)

(E102) Go R 300 yds to crossroads & turn L.

(E103) Go .5 mile, pass steel shed L & cross cattle grid.

(E104) Turn R & follow R hedge (via bust gate) to join track & take gate. Go R, round L bend & follow track .6 mile to lane.

(E105) Go R .35 mile to drive L (Garegllywd), & take R of 2 gates.

(W264) Go R 350 yds & take
take slip road L.

(W265) Approach house but
go R past red barns & join
grey track. Go .75 mile to
pass house L & meet lane.

(W266) Cross lane, climb
steps & cross stile. Go
ahead to join & follow R
hedge to its corner.

(W267) Go R, bearing L to
finger post. Follow hedge
up field, bearing L from
it to take midfence gate.

(W268) Follow path & cross
stile. Bear L up field
[brg 216] & (when in view)
follow top fence to finger
post, & cross stile.

(W269) Follow path through
bracken (ignore R forks)
up to fingerpost [brg
186]. Go R & take gate.

(W270) Go ahead to gate &
cross stile. Go on a few
paces to finger post &
gate L. DON'T GO THROUGH.

(W271) Put your back to
gate, go half R [brg 328]
& pick up faint track to
rock with white marble
inset. ▶

(E96) Go with rocks on
your R & find track again.
Swing R through end of
rocks, then follow line of
faint track UP for 150 yds
[brg 173] to finger post
by gate.

(E97) DON'T TAKE GATE, go
L to next gates & cross
stile. Go ahead till track
bends R & take gate ahead.

(E98) Go ahead 200 yds to
finger post. Go half L on
path through bracken (take
either fork, they rejoin)
to finger post, & cross
stile.

(E99) Go half R to just
above trees & cross mid-
fence stile. Follow path &
take gate.

(E100) Bear L & go para-
llel with L hedge to field
end. Go R by bottom hedge
to corner, then L down
hedge to stile & lane.

(E101) Cross & take gate
R. Pass house & follow
green track .75 mile, then
through farm & up slip
road to A44. ◀

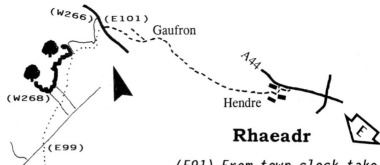

(W266) (E101) Gaufron

A44

Hendre

Rhaeadr

(W272) Follow track L through rocks, bearing up L to find clear track. Follow down to gorse patch & go R down to gate. Follow clear track/trough .3 mile down to A470.

(W273) Go R 50 yds, cross road & take stile. Go down hedge & cross stile to fenced path. Follow it to cross stile & bridge.

(W274) Follow river for 2 fields & cross stile onto fenced path. Go to A470.

(W275) Go L up to town centre.

Rhaeadr

(E91) From town clock take South Street .3 mile. Cross river, pass white house R & take small wooden gate to fenced path

(E92) Follow to stile & field. Follow river via 2 bridges & cross stile. Follow fenced path & cross stile. Go up with hedge on your R & cross stile to A470.

(E93) Cross, go R 50 yds & take gate L. Follow stream 150 yds & take green track L, ignore green top posts.

(E94) Follow track parallel with L fence to stone wall L. Go R across hillside & take gate.

(E95) Track goes up to gorse patch, turns L to gorse & rock clump, then vanishes.

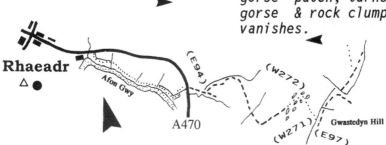

Rhaeadr
△ ●

Afon Gwy

A470

(E94) (W272)

(W271) (E97)

Gwastedyn Hill

Rhaeadr

(W276) From town clock take West Street. Cross river plus 100yds (past 1st road L), & take 2nd.

(W277) Cross to churchyard gate & enter. Go ahead to far corner & take kissing gate. Follow R hedge up to field corner & take kissing gate. Go L to lane

(W278) Go ahead .3 mile to sharp L bend & take track ahead. Follow it .5 mile to crosstracks.

(W279) Go L past sheds, swing R to near old bridge but take gated track L. Follow it .35 mile to lane

(W280) Go R 400 yds to farm. Take gated track L to river & cross bridge. (Easier if you sort of boogie across.) ►

(E87) Go R & join track up to gate & lane by farm. Go R 400 yds & take track L.

(E88) Go .35 mile & take gate. Go R, curve L past sheds & take gate onto crosstracks.

(E89) Go R .5 mile to lane. Go ahead .3 mile to R bend & take rising track L.

(E90) Take kissing gate, go down L fence & take kissing gate to church-yard. Go ahead & take gate to road. Go ahead to B4518, then R to town centre.

Rhaeadr

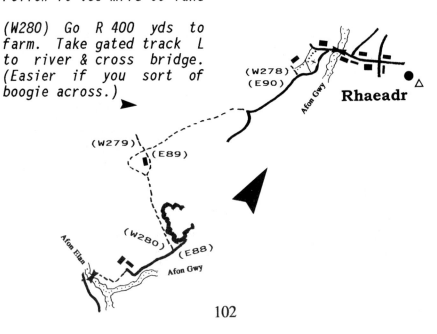

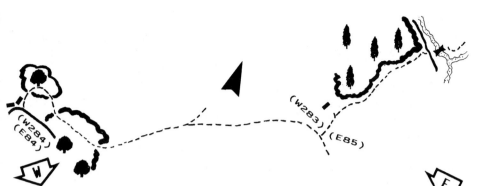

(W281) Go R up to lane. Go L 50 yds & take grass track R. Take L of 2 gates

(W282) Go .6 mile up to house R, & join track going ahead to main track.

(W283) Go R 1.5 miles & meet lane.

(W284) Go R 400 yds & take lane L. Follow tarmac .5 mile to its end, & take gate.

(W285) Go ahead on stone track (ignore grass track bearing L) for 375 yds, to markpost & faint path L.

[FOR VIEWS of reservoirs and dams follow track ahead, then return.]

[FOR VIEWS of reservoirs and dams go L, and then return.]

(E83) Go R 300 yds to gate & lane. Go .5 mile down to T junction. Go R 400 yards to Talwrn Lodge & join rising track L.

(E84) Go .9 mile, (through wood & across moor) to fork. Go R .6 mile & take 1st track L.

(E85) Pass house gate & go down by fence .6 mile to lane.

(E86) Go L 50 yds to end of garden fence & take gate R. Follow path down & cross bridge (easy if you sort of boogie across).

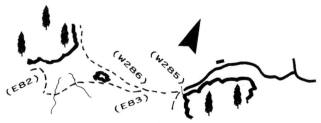

103

(W286) Follow faint path L past L side of ruin, cross 2 streams & swing R to corner of forest.

(W287) Follow green track by trees .7 mile, to cross ford & take gate.

(W288) Cross 2 fords & follow track across open hillside to take gate. Cross ford & join stone track.

(W289) Follow it .75 mile, to cross ford & take gate.

(W290) Go ahead .3 mile to far end of farm sheds.

Llanerch

[TO REACH PHONE BOX & road go ahead across bridge.

IF STARTING from phone box take side lane to 1st farm shed.]

(W291) Go up to front of shed & take tarmac lane .5 mile to farm.

(W292) Pass black shed on your R & follow stone track .3 mile to junction. ▶

(E76) Go downstream & pick up rough wet track. Follow 2 miles to pass black shed by farm, & join lane.

(E77) Go .5 mile to face barn & turn L down onto to lane.

Llanerch

[TO REACH PHONE BOX & road go L over bridge.

IF STARTING from phone box take side lane to 1st farm shed.]

(E78) Go through farm (past R forks) & follow riverside track .3 mile to cross ford.

(E79) Ignore track L, take rising fork R. Follow stone track .75 mile to its end, & take gate.

(E80) Follow grass track across open hillside & through 2 fords to take gate.

(E81) Continue on track by trees .7 mile to forest corner.

(E82) Follow track R to cross 2 streams, pass ruin in plantation & go up to join track from L. ◀

(W293) Take track R (riverside) for 1.7 mile to near dam, then go L up tributary & cross bridge.

(W294) Take small gate & go ahead via stile & small gate to join track. Go R & cross river.

Claerwen Dam

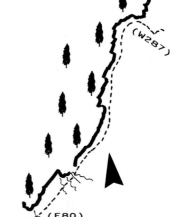

(W287)

(E80)
(W289)

(W290)

(E79)

(E77)
(W292)

Llanerch

Claerwen Dam

(E73) From small car park at top of dam, take iron kissing gate & follow path down to road.

(E74) Cross bridge & take gate. Go half R towards house & take gate. Turn L to L side of shed & take small gate.

(E75) Go ahead via stile & small gate to cross foot-bridge. Go L to meet Afon Claerwen & curve R.

Claerwen Dam

(E74)

(E76)

(W293)

Claerwen Dam

(W295) From roadway side of bridge below dam, go half L & take iron kissing gate. Follow rising path to road.

(W296) Go L, DON'T CROSS DAM, & follow waterside stone track 6 miles. Pass head of lake & farm, & cross timber bridge.

(W297) Continue on stone track 2 miles to junction, & join tarmac lane.◄

(W298) Go ahead 2.75 miles to big, sloping roofed building L, with lane opposite (Glanpond).

Ffair Rhos

[FOR FFAIR RHOS continue along road 1.5 miles.]

►

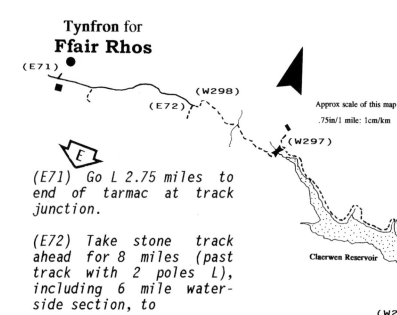

Tynfron for
Ffair Rhos
(E71)

(W298)
(E72)

Approx scale of this map
.75in/1 mile: 1cm/km

(W297)

Claerwen Reservoir

(W296)

Claerwen Dam

(E71) Go L 2.75 miles to end of tarmac at track junction.

(E72) Take stone track ahead for 8 miles (past track with 2 poles L), including 6 mile waterside section, to

Claerwen Dam
◄

Claerwen Dam

(E69) Go L by L fence to field corner. Go R by fence .35 mile to meet track, & take gate L.

(E70) Follow 3 miles:
- *across boggy bit*
- *past rising track L*
- *past ruined farm*
- *past farm L on sharp R bend*
- *past 2 more ruins*
- *L at fork*
to T junction at road.

Ffair Rhos ◀

[Ffair Rhos is R 1.5 mile]

Bridell

Blaen Marchnant

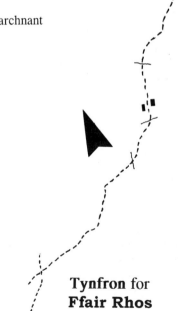

Tynfron for
Ffair Rhos

(W299) Take lane R (soon becomes track) & follow for 3 miles:
- *at junction go R*
- *pass farm R on sharp L bend (Blaen Marchnant)*
- *pass ruin R (Bridell) & take gate*
- *WATCH for next gate*
- *cross boggy bit (may be best to cross fence L) then climb, round L bend with track on bare rock, & take next gate.*

(W300) Go R by fence .35 mile to field corner with gate R. DON'T TAKE IT. ▶

(W300)

(E70)

(W299)

(W301) Go L on rough track by R fence 300yds, to lone trees. Go R with fence on your R to field corner, & take fence gap onto track.

(W302) Cross track & go ahead, bearing L to join rough track. Curve L & down to take gate. Follow fenced track 350 yds (past ruin) to join lane.

(W303) Go ahead 350 yds (past track R) to stone shed L, & cross stile opposite.

(W304) Go ahead, pass projecting fence corner L, follow fence to field corner & cross stile.

(W305) Follow green path bearing L through gorse to grass field edge. Go down 20 paces & cross (bust?) stile L. Follow fenced path to lane.

(W306) Go R 150 yds & take track R. Go 50 paces & cross stile L.

(W307) Go ahead 50 yds, then turn half R & cross stile onto bend of lane.

(W308) Go ahead past drive R to fork & take track ahead (Gwarcwm). Go 50 paces & turn L to house.▶

(E64) Go half L to pass R side of house, climb bank & cross stile onto track. Go R to lane junction.

(E65) Go L up to 1st house L & on its far side take fenced path L. Go to end & cross (bust?) stile L.

(E66) Go R on faint path 28 paces, take path through gorse & on to cross stile. Go ahead by R fence to its corner, then keep ahead up to stile & lane.

(E67) Go L 350 yds (past track L) to junction. Take track R, round L bend, pass ruin & take gate.

(E68) Follow rough track curving R. When it vanishes bear L by fence to field corner with gate L. Go ahead across track & through fence gap. Follow L fence to its corner & join track. ◀

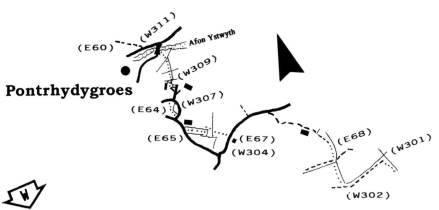

Pontrhydygroes

(W309) Go R past front of building & cross stile. Go ahead by R fence & cross stile. Go ahead down green path, curving L to cross stile & reach road at

Pontrhydygroes

[Miner's Arms 300 yds L.]

(W310) FROM TREGARON side of river bridge cross to Devil's Bridge side. Go L 150 yds to speed limit sign, & climb (overgrown?) sloping path R.

(W311) Go up 20 paces with stream on your R, then cross it as soon as you can & climb R bank.

(W312) Walk along bank by sunken track for 100 yds then, as soon as you can, go down to walk in it.

(E60) Follow line of track 100 yds & at the obvious place go R across stream. Go L down to road. Go L down to bridge.

Pontrhydygroes

[Miners' Arms across bridge plus 300 yds.]

(E61) From Tregaron side of river bridge take steep rising path on R of gate, & cross stile.

(E62) Follow green path up to cross stile. Follow L fence & cross stile.

(E63) Go ahead 40 paces to front of house & turn L between hedges to track. Go R & join lane. Go ahead to R bend, climb steps & cross stile.

109

(W313) Go 450 yds (round R bend & across track between fields) but when track ahead is blocked, go R through gap into field.

(W314) Follow line of track & take gate. Go ahead on track, pass farm on your R, & round L bend plus 100 yds to 2 gates.

(W315) Take R gate (bust?) or cross fence, & follow line of track up field & through gate. Track goes on as reedy trough with fence R for .5 mile, to field corner with gates

(W316) Take gate ahead, cross stream, follow track & take gate. Go ahead past house to gate & B4343.

(W317) Go L .6 mile, KEEP TO L side of road to 1st house. Cross & walk on R verge to 2nd house. Return to L side to 3rd house.

(W318) Take track R, pass house & take gate. Go ahead by L fence & follow rough track to take gate.

(W319) Follow track with trees L, curving L to take gate by sheds. Go up to crest (past track L), then down to tip of forest.

(E54) Follow rough track ahead to field corner & take gate. Go ahead to B4343. CARE.

(E55) CROSS ROAD & go L on verge to 1st house. Cross & walk L verge to 2nd house. Cross road & follow R side to 3rd house.

(E56) Enter steel gate R & go ahead through next gate. Follow fenced track down & take gate.

(E57) Go ahead .5 mile by old track (reedy trough by L fence) to gate L. IF track blocked ahead take gate L, follow line of track & cross gate or fence onto earth track.

(E58) Go L, round R bend to pass farm on your L, then curved shed, & take gate. Follow track 50 yds, but where track bends L, take gate ahead into field

(E59) Follow bushes R a few paces & as soon as you can, enter track R. Go 450 yds (across track between fields & round L bend). When track becomes wet, climb path up L bank.

**Pontarfynach/
Devil's Bridge**

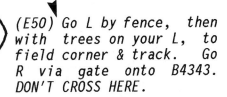

(W323)

(E51)

(W321)
(E52)

(E49) From gate of station
cross road & take track L
of Post Office. At fork
go R up to gate, & cross
stile R.▼

W

(W320) Take track L by
trees 1.4 miles to B4343.

(W321) Go R 20 paces,
cross to L side of road &
pass lane & house L. Cross
to R side, pass two houses
to corner & take green
track R.

(W322) Take gate &   go
ahead to 5 yards from next
field corner. Turn L off
track & keep trees on your
R, then fence, to cross
stile R.

(W323) Go L on track to
A4120 at

(W320)
(E53)

(E50) Go L by fence, then
with trees on your L, to
field corner & track.   Go
R via gate onto B4343.
DON'T CROSS HERE.

**Pontarfynach/
Devil's Bridge**

(E51) Go L to last house,
cross road & follow it
past house & lane R. CARE.
Stay on same side to near
bend, then switch to L &
take track L

(E52) Go 1.4 mile (via
gates & through forest) to
tip of forest &   stone
track.

(E58)
(W315)

(W314) (E59)

Pontrhydygroes

Afon Ystwyth

(E53) Go R up to crest,
pass track R, go down to
farm R & take gate. Follow
curving track to forest
111 edge & take gate. ◄

Rhaeadr (or Rhaeadr Gwy) translates into English as 'waterfall on the Afon Gwy'. Most of the falls were destroyed in 1780 to build the road bridge, but what remains is still impressive. This is a market town for the region, but also a tiny oasis of facilities in the vast, empty countryside of mid Wales. You will find barely another settlement of more than a few houses between Llanwrtyd Wells and Llanidloes, Llandrindod Wells and Pontrhydfendigaid. Rhaeadr feels like a frontier town.

The **Elan Valley Reservoirs** were Birmingham's answer in the 1880s to the bursting, bustling, prosperous city's demand for water. Supplies from local rivers and wells were proving insufficient and unwholesome. The idea was so simple that it has the quality of genius. Bring the abundant surplus water from the great, green sponge of mid Wales down a pipe to Birmingham, and since Wales is higher than central England it will flow downhill all the way.

Cwm Elan was flooded by three stone dams in the early 1900s and the works opened in 1907. The Claerwen Dam is clad with stone but it is actually a concrete dam built in the 1950s and retains a vastly greater volume of water than the others. The aqueduct or pipeline is 73 miles long with a fall of 169 feet. There are 36 miles of tunnels and covered canals and the rest is pipeline. The water crosses seven large valleys, including the Teme and the Severn.

Hafod. Some 150 yards east of the bridge at Pontrhydy-groes is a grand gateway. This was one of the entrances to the incredible Hafod, a great house built in the 1780s which stood about a mile up the Ystwyth valley. The story is told in full by Elizabeth Inglis Jones in *Peacocks In Paradise* (Faber). Lack of space limits what I can say, but the house was in parts a gothic tower, a Moorish dome and a Grecian villa. In the grounds were lawns, miles of ornamental walks, bridges and grottos, waterfalls and statues, peacocks and marble. It may have been the inspiration for Coleridge's poem Kubla Khan, a sort of old time Itchycoo Park.

The **Vale of Rheidol Railway** was opened in 1902 to serve local metal mines and attract tourists, and tourist traffic on the 12 mile trip has always supported the line. The Cambrian Railway Company bought it, but in 1923 it became part of the Great Western Railway and in 1948 of British Railways. The very narrow gauge of 1 foot 11.5 inches was the smallest possible which would give a reasonable carrying capacity and yet cope with the fierce curves. The three steam engines weigh 25 tons each and are about 8 feet wide. They and the coaches were built at Swindon by the GWR in the late 1920s. Gradients are severe, involving a climb from 4 metres above sea level to 209 metres.

Nanteos Mansion is now a comfortable hotel standing in ample, well tended parkland, but a house may well have stood here for as long as there has been civilization in Wales. The monks of Strata Florida certainly thought it was a safe place to leave their most precious relic, the Cwpan, or Cup. This was said to be the Holy Grail which in some manner found its way to the great Cistercian Monastery. It was at Nanteos from the 1530s and was occasionally lent to people for purposes of healing until 1903. The present house was built and the parkland laid out in 1739 by Thomas Powell.

Vale of Rheidol Railway

Pontarfynach/
Devil's Bridge

(W324) Face gate to station & go L .3 mile. Stay on L side to Mount Pleasant, then switch to R side to pass last house, & take gate R.

(W325) Go ahead to mark-post, then curve L beside trees & take earth track L

(W326) Pass R fork & follow path above railway, then falling to follow it. Cross stile onto line.

(W327) Go L 15 paces & take small gate R. Follow path & cross stile onto line again.

(W328) Go R 33 paces & cross stile L. Go R on path & cross stile onto line. Go ahead & cross stile onto path.

(W329) Go down 400 yds to join green track from R. Go L to gate & stile at wood edge. DON'T CROSS.

(W330) Turn sharp L up steep grass path to fence corner. Go R by fence 200 yds to join track by gate.

(W331) Go ahead .5 mile (via gate) to pass falling R fork & take gate. ▶

(E42) Go R 350 yds (path rises & becomes stone track) to where track ahead is suddenly mossy, & take steep path R.

(E43) Go up (via zig zags) to cross stile, railway & stile.

(E44) Follow path & cross stile onto line. Go R 33 paces & cross stile L. Follow path & take small gate onto railway. Go L 16 paces & cross stile R.

(E45) Go L by fence & take small gate. Follow steep path up & through woodland to join wide grass track.

(E46) Go ahead, pass small rising earth path R & curve R round side of hill into field.

(E47) Go R round edge of trees, then pass R end of houses & take gate onto A4120.

(E48) Go L on L side of road to Mount Pleasant, then cross to R side into

Pontarfynach/
◀ Devil's Bridge

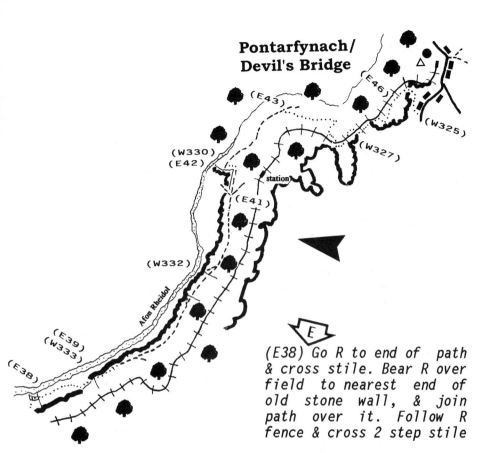

Pontarfynach/
Devil's Bridge

(E43)
(E46)
(W325)
(W330)
(E42)
(W327)
station
(E41)
(W332)
Afon Rheidol
(E39)
(W333)
(E38)

W

(W332) Go on .5 mile & cross stile into field.

(W333) Go ahead on top of bank to pass old walls, then turn half R towards blue bridge. Pass close to weir & cross stile.

(W334) Follow fenced path to picnic site & cross 1st stile L. Go R on faint grass path & pass ruin on your L.

E

(E38) Go R to end of path & cross stile. Bear R over field to nearest end of old stone wall, & join path over it. Follow R fence & cross 2 step stile

(E39) Follow path .5 mile (via gate) to pass L fork & take upper of 2 gates.

(E40) WATCH. Go .35 mile, then ignore steep rising track R & take gap on R of gate ahead.

(E41) Follow L fence 200 yds to its corner, then L down steep path to meet path & gate L. DON'T GO THROUGH.

(W335) Follow line of L fence & green track between fence & trees. Detour past fallen trees, join rising earth track & take gate.

(W336) Follow stone/earth track .5 mile to pass dam & meet bend of lane.

(W337) Go ahead 1.5 mile (past lane L & over crossroads) to sharp L bend, & take gated stone track R (G R Smith).

(W338) Follow stone track .4 mile (across railway) into ex farmyard.

(W339) Go ahead past short green track & take gate. Follow faint green path parallel with railway. Pass trees on your L, go through grove of trees, curve L & take small gate into wood.

(W340) Cross stream, turn sharp R & follow earth track 250 yds to junction with stone path. ▶

(E33) Follow path, curving R across field & through grove of trees. Curve L into field, then go parallel with railway & take gate into ex farmyard

(E34) Go L through gate & follow stone track .4 mile (across railway) to lane.

(E35) Go L 1.3 mile:
 - past farm drive R
 - over crossroads
 - past rising lane R
 to sharp L bend by dam, & take track ahead.

(E36) Go .5 mile. WATCH:
 - pass falling green
                track L,
 - rising track R &
 - falling track L,
 then take NEXT falling track L (with gate in view) & take gate.

(E37) Go down to field. Keep R & pass fallen trees, then bear up R to join green track. Follow R fence to its corner. Pass ruin on your R, curve L to green bridge & cross either of 2 stiles onto fenced path. ◀

116

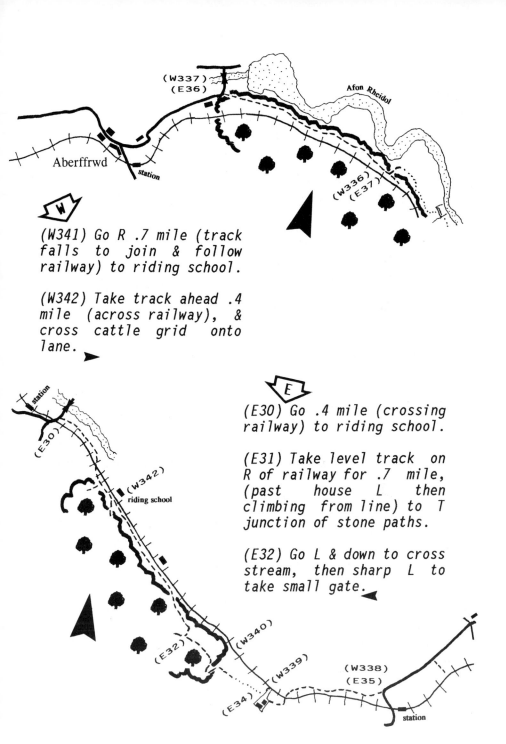

(W337)
(E36)

Afon Rheidol

Aberffrwd

station

(W336)
(E37)

W

(W341) Go R .7 mile (track falls to join & follow railway) to riding school.

(W342) Take track ahead .4 mile (across railway), & cross cattle grid onto lane.

station

(E30)

E

(E30) Go .4 mile (crossing railway) to riding school.

(W342)

riding school

(E31) Take level track on R of railway for .7 mile, (past house L then climbing from line) to T junction of stone paths.

(E32) Go L & down to cross stream, then sharp L to take small gate.

(E32)

(W340)

(W339)

(W338)
(E35)

(E34)

station

117

(W343) Cross railway, pass lane L, & go .4 mile to take farm track L.

(W344) Pass through farmyard & go L up stone track (past white house) to take gate. Go on 250 yds to end of track & take gate ahead

(W345) Go ahead & take next (bust?) gate. Follow R fence down into hollow & up into field. Head for top R field corner, & on L side of tree clump find gate. DON'T GO THROUGH.

(W346) Go R 25 paces & turn L through trees into field. Pass ruin on your R & follow line of trees to take small gate ahead. Follow R fence & take steel gate onto A4120.

(W347) Go R 250 yds to school at

Capel Seion

(W348) From school take lane beside it, go round L bend & take gate R. Pass shed & bear R to follow R fence. Pass 1st gate R, enter next field & take 2nd gate R. ▶

(E23) Go R by fence to field corner & cross fence. Go L along fence around field edge to field corner with 2 gates.

(E24) Take gate ahead. Go L via fence gap, head for R end of shed & take gate onto lane. Go L to A4120,

Capel Seion

(E25) From end of lane by school, go R on A4120 for 250 yds. Pass last house L & take 2nd field gate L.

(E26) Follow L hedge & take small midfence gate. Go ahead with trees/bank on your L past ruin, then curve R through tree clump into next field. Go R to edge of clump by gate.

(E27) Go half R to bottom fence by trees. Follow fence R into hollow then up track, & take gate.

(E28) Take gate ahead onto track & follow it down through farm to lane.

(E29) Go R .4 mile (past lane R) to cross railway & take track beside it. ◀

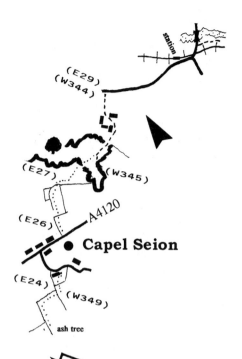

(W349) Follow R fence &
round field corner to
lone ash tree. Cross fence
R & follow R fence to
field corner by wood.

(W350) Go L down wood edge
to bottom field corner &
take gate R. Follow wood
edge past cottage, take
gate & follow stone track
to crossways.

(W351) Go ahead to house.
Go L past it to gate &
cross stile. Go R by wall/
fence to field corner. Go
L with fence on your R to
field corner, then cross
stile & footbridge.

(W352) Go half R between
tree clumps to far top
field corner [brg 213], &
cross stile to B4340.
GREAT CARE. ▶

(E20) Go half R [brg 33]
between tree clumps to
bottom R field corner, &
cross footbridge L.

(E21) Cross stile & follow
L fence to field corner.
Go R by fence/wall to gate
& cross stile. Go ahead
up to stone track. Go R to
crossways.

(E22) Go ahead & take gate
into field. Follow wood
edge to field corner &
take gate. Go L up wood
edge to field corner gate.
DON'T GO THROUGH. ◀

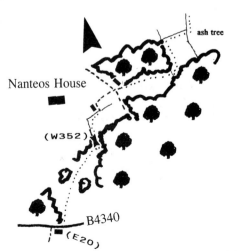

119

(W353) Cross road, go R 100 yds & pass house drive to take gate L. Follow green track up 180 yds to gateways. Go R 150 yds to near house, & take gate L.

(W354) Go R to field corner, turn L on old track 100 yds & take gate.

(W355) Go R to field corner, turn L, follow R fence .35 mile (via gate) & take gate onto bend of lane.

(W356) Go R .75 mile (past gates of golf course & Penlleine) & cross stile L into small grove of trees.

(W357) Go half L across field corner & cross stile. Go R by fence to end of trees & cross stile.

(E15) Go R .75 mile (past gates of Penlleine & golf course & under power lines) to sharp R bend with gates ahead & L. Take gate L.

(E16) Follow L fence (via gate) & join track down to field corner. Go R 100 yds to bend & turn L through 2nd of 2 gates.

(E17) Follow track down to field corner, turn R past house & take gate L.

(E18) Go R on track to field corner. Go down L & take gate onto B4340. DON'T CROSS HERE.

(E19) Go R 100 yds, CROSS ROAD WITH CARE & cross stile.

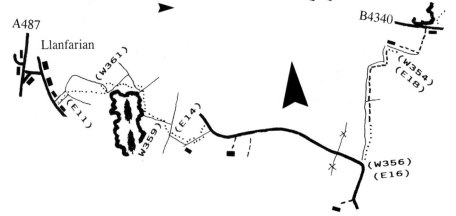

120

(W358) Follow fence past 1st field corner to 2nd, & take gate ahead. Go half R across field corner & take gate.

(W359) Go L down fence & around field edge by trees to R end of wood, & cross stile. Go half L across field corner & cross stile

(W360) Go half R, but circle L round small hill & cross stile. Go down across field corner & cross 2 stiles.

(W361) Go L along terrace to field corner & turn sharp R. Pass lone mid-field tree to bottom field corner, & cross stile.

(W362) Follow fenced path down to lane. Go R, pass 1st road L & take 2nd L down to A487 at Llanfarian

▶

(E9) Cross, go R & take road L. Pass road R & go up to T junction.

(E10) Go R 300yds to pass Hillview Croft & take fenced path L. Go up & cross stile into field.

(E11) Go half R up gorsey hillside to NEAREST TIP of wood R [Brg 87]. Go L by field top fence 25 yds & cross twin stiles.

(E12) Go half R across field corner & cross midfence stile. Go half L, but circle R round small hill & cross stile.

(E13) Go half R to end of trees & cross stile. Go R around field edge to top field corner & take gate. Go half L across field corner & take gate.

(E14) Follow R fence, go round next field corner & cross stile. Follow fence/ bank 50 yds & cross stile L. Go half R across field corner & cross stile onto lane. ◀◀

(W363) Cross road, go R & take road L (Bryn Egeur). Go to R bend & cross stile ahead. Go ahead by R fence & cross stile.

(W364) Follow path & take kissing gate. Follow R fence to houses & cross stile. Go ahead, cross lane & take stone track to field.

(W365) Follow L fence to field corner & cross stile L. Follow fence round R bend & down to cross stile.

(W366) Follow fenced path to lane. Go R to road. Go L across bridge, then turn R & cross stile onto fenced stone track.

(W367) Go 1.25 mile, take gate & go ahead onto shingle bank.

THAT'S IT REALLY

►

(E4) Turn L, follow shingle bank .4 mile to cross strange concrete thingy, then turn L & take gate.

(E5) Follow fenced track 1.25 mile to gate, & cross stile.

(E6) Go ahead to road. Go L over bridge then R on lane. Pass house L, & take steps L.

(E7) Follow fenced path & cross stile. Go L up fence & follow it round corner to cross stile. Go R by fence & join track to lane.

(E8) Cross & take small steel gate. Follow edge of trees & take kissing gate. Follow path & cross stile. Follow L fence & cross stile to road. Go ahead down to A487.

◄◄

(W368) *Go R to harbour &*
cross bridge R. Go 100 yds
to R bend & turn L down
track. Pass boathouse &
flats on your R, then
follow red blocked water-
side path to end of 3
arched stone bridge.

(W369) *Go L to seek the*
highlife & naughty places
of Aberystwyth, & let me
know if you find any.

Aberystwyth

(E1) *Find junction of Heol*
y Bont (Bridge St) & Dan
Dre (Mill St) on A487 by
stone bridge over Afon
Rheidol.

(E2) *Cross R side of*
bridge to end of stone
parapet & turn sharp R.
Head for riverbank &
follow red blocked water-
side path for .4 mile to
its end, at end of road L.

(E3) *Go ahead to pass*
flats on your L, then
boathouse, & bear R to
meet lane. Go R & cross
bridge.

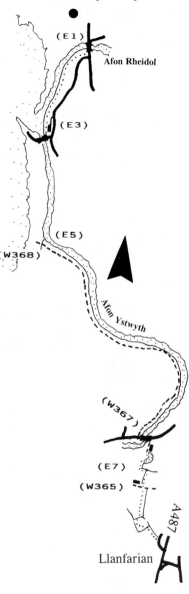

Aberystwyth

(E1)

Afon Rheidol

(E3)

(E5)

(W368)

Afon Ystwyth

(W367)

(E7)

(W365)

A487

Llanfarian

◄◄◄
123

You approach **Aberystwyth** beside the Afon Ystwyth and your final, triumphal, entry is stumbling along a shingle bank barely out of reach of the roaring Irish Sea. Like as not, a shrieking wind will be pelting you with horizontal sleet, but I know you wouldn't have it any other way.

In Aberystwyth the longest cliff railway in Britain up Constitution Hill will take you to to the biggest Camera Obscura in the world. From here you can look through a 14 inch lens over land and sea in a 360 degree sweep, if this is what you like to do. Then there is the Norman Castle, the University College of Wales, the National Library of Wales and a Theological College. There it sits on the sea front, massive with rectitude, grey with spirituality, facing a tacky, giggling pier. In this gateway to hell theology students can pass sinful hours in the amusement arcade, snooker hall and social club - *'Drinkin and dancing until 2am on Fridays'*.

The first castle was built in about 1110 some 1.5 miles from the present site, and this was at the mouth of the Ystwyth. What you see are the remains of Edward I's stonghold built in 1277. The site is a rocky headland surrounded by the sea or marshland, and it could be supplied by sea. It last saw military action during the Civil War. From 1637 the castle housed a mint making silver coins for Charles I from local metal, but the Royalist garrison surrendered in 1646.

Here on the sea front is the war memorial. On the tip of a slender column floats a slender lady in a filmy dress who, for some reason, is balanced by one foot on a sphere. She is chucking into the sea a circular object, which is not a lifebelt, but a wreath. Imagine the thoughts of the shipwrecked mariner who had been hoping for a lifebelt. At the base of the monument and trying to escape the embrace of some lascivious seaweed is a breathtakingly massive young lady. Bronzily bare and amply breasted, her eyes are on the horizon. She is thinking of sailors and would like to succour them. Blast the seaweed.